HEART CRY

Searching for Answers in a
World Without Meaning

JILL BRISCOE

NAVPRESS®

BRINGING TRUTH TO LIFE

OUR GUARANTEE TO YOU

We believe so strongly in the message of our books that we
are making this quality guarantee to you. If for any reason
you are disappointed with the content of this book, return
the title page to us with your name and address and we will
refund to you the list price of the book. To help us serve you
better, please briefly describe why you were disappointed.
Mail your refund request to: NavPress, P.O. Box 35002,
Colorado Springs, CO 80935.

The Navigators is an international Christian organization. Our mission is to advance the gospel of Jesus and His kingdom into the nations through spiritual generations of laborers living and discipling among the lost. We see a vital movement of the gospel, fueled by prevailing prayer, flowing freely through relational networks and out into the nations where workers for the kingdom are next door to everywhere.

NavPress is the publishing ministry of The Navigators. The mission of NavPress is to reach, disciple, and equip people to know Christ and make Him known by publishing life-related materials that are biblically rooted and culturally relevant. Our vision is to stimulate spiritual transformation through every product we publish.

ISBN-10: 1-57683-981-8
ISBN-13: 978-1-57683-981-2

Cover design by Arvid Wallen
Cover photo by Inmagine
Creative Team: Rachelle Gardner, Arvid Wallen, Pat Reinheimer

Some of the anecdotal illustrations in this book are true to life and are included with the permission of the persons involved. All other illustrations are composites of real situations, and any resemblance to people living or dead is coincidental.

Unless otherwise identified, all Scripture quotations in this publication are taken from the *HOLY BIBLE: NEW INTERNATIONAL VERSION*® (NIV®). Copyright © 1973, 1978, 1984 by International Bible Society. Used by permission of Zondervan Publishing House. All rights reserved. Other versions used include: the *Holy Bible, New Living Translation* (NLT), copyright 1996. Used by permission of Tyndale House Publishers, Inc., Wheaton, Illinois 60189. All rights reserved; *THE MESSAGE* (MSG). Copyright © by Eugene H. Peterson 1993, 1994, 1995, 1996, 2000, 2001, 2002. Used by permission of NavPress Publishing Group; and the *King James Version* (KJV).

All poems written by Jill Briscoe unless otherwise identified. "Heaven," "Give My Words Wings," and "Don't Waste the Pain" originally published in *God's Front Door* by Jill Briscoe, Monarch Books, © 2004. Used by permission.

"Overtime" (chapter 2) adapted from an essay originally published in *The Garden of Grace* by Jill Briscoe, Monarch Books, © 2004. Used by permission.

Published in association with the literary agency of Alive Communications, Inc.,7680 Goddard Street, Suite 200, Colorado Springs, Colorado, 80920.

Briscoe, Jill.
  Heart cry : searching for answers in a world without meaning / Jill Briscoe.
    p. cm.
  Includes bibliographical references.
  ISBN-13: 978-1-57683-981-2
  ISBN-10: 1-57683-981-8
  1. Bible. O.T. Ecclesiastes--Criticism, interpretation, etc. I. Title.

BS1475.52.B75 2006
223'.806--dc22

2007010042

Printed in the United States of America
1 2 3 4 5 6 7 8 / 11 10 09 08 07

FOR A FREE CATALOG OF NAVPRESS BOOKS & BIBLE STUDIES,
CALL 1-800-366-7788 (USA) OR 1-800-839-4769 (CANADA).

Dedicated to all God's wise men and women who have

spoken truth into my life at the right time,

in the right way, for the right reasons. Thank you.

CONTENTS

Acknowledgment   9
INTRODUCTION: Is This All There Is?   11

CHAPTER 1: Searching for Significance   17
  In a Put-Me-Down World

CHAPTER 2: Searching for Sense   35
  In a World Gone Mad

CHAPTER 3: Searching for a Song   53
  In a World of Tears

CHAPTER 4: Searching for Satisfaction   73
  In a Sex-Saturated World

CHAPTER 5: Searching for Salvation   91
  In a Lost World

CHAPTER 6: Searching for a Soul Mate   111
  In a Lonely World

CHAPTER 7: Searching for Social Justice   129
  In an Unjust World

CHAPTER 8: Searching for Speaking Skills   149
  That Will Change My World

CHAPTER 9: Searching for Security   169
  In an Unsafe World

Notes   191
About the Author   195

ACKNOWLEDGMENT

Thank you to Rachelle Gardner, who somehow kept the book on track through not a few difficulties, kept my voice, and read my heart, editing masterfully.

IS THIS ALL THERE IS?

Now all has been heard;
here is the conclusion of the matter:

Fear God and keep his commandments,
for this is the whole duty of man.

ECCLESIASTES 12:13

As I prepared to delve into the book of Ecclesiastes and share with you the results of my study, I couldn't help but think of a time years ago when my husband Stuart and I worked at a short-term Bible school. A young Japanese student—whose English was anything but fluent—gave a talk on King Solomon, author of the books of Proverbs, Ecclesiastes, and Song of Songs. The student began by saying he wanted to draw some lessons from the life of Solomon who "had seven hundred wives and three hundred cucumbers." His talk was quite interesting! It's a bit much when you think of all those wives and "cucumbers" isn't it? And then to read that Solomon was the wisest man who ever lived?

God had promised Solomon, "I will give you a wise and discerning heart, so that there will never have been anyone like you, nor will there ever be" (1 Kings 3:12). Yet here was this man living an unwise and profligate life. Solomon had fallen away from the Lord by disobeying God's rules for kings—namely the multiplying of wives, horses, and gold against the Lord's explicit instructions. He played the fool, only returning to his senses and regaining wisdom after decades of self-indulgent living. In his twilight years, he learned that only God can give purpose and meaning to life. Solomon wrote the book of Ecclesiastes so that we won't have to spend our own lives going down the wrong paths as he did. We already have the answer: In God alone will our hearts find rest.

There has been debate over the years about the authorship of Ecclesiastes, but most scholars believe it was indeed King David's son Solomon. The book opens with a fitting description of Solomon:

"The words of the Teacher, son of David, king in Jerusalem." Verse 12 reads, "I, the Teacher, was king over Israel in Jerusalem." The author describes himself as "wiser than any other leader"—a portrayal typically attributed to King Solomon. In the opening two chapters of Ecclesiastes, the Teacher's autobiographical remarks speak of a lifestyle of such wealth and opulence that only *this* son of David—Solomon himself—could be the person involved.

The word "Ecclesiastes" is a Greek translation of the Hebrew *Qoheleth*, which means "Teacher." Solomon is the Teacher, or Qoheleth. I will be using the words Teacher and Qoheleth throughout the next chapters, referring to Solomon.

One thing that gives some pause as to the book's authorship is in the last chapter, where it sounds somewhat self-serving for Solomon to say about himself: "Not only was the Teacher wise, but also he imparted knowledge to the people" (12:9). Some commentators say this was a postscript written by a disciple or scribe as he edited the writing for publication. Others would understandably question how we can call someone "wise" who marries seven hundred women and acquires three hundred concubines!

Nevertheless, it seems to be true that Solomon is the author. So perhaps further details about Solomon, his surroundings, and his relationship to God will assist us as we wrestle with the importance of this marvelous book.

Solomon's world looked frighteningly similar to the world in which we live: at every turn, Solomon saw spite, scandal, and self-centeredness. Although his court officials were supposed to dispense justice, they grew distracted by selfish interests. His city's marketplace leaders had become corrupt. Outrageous violence threatened to overtake his people. And he had nobody to blame but himself: his own failures as a king overshadowed even the worst evil in his people. He had overindulged—in wine, in women, in worldly pursuits—and had hoarded his life's gains for his own pleasure instead of using it for good.

Ecclesiastes, then, is a testimony of one man's erratic trek back and forth along the continuum where one end is foolishness, the other wisdom. This little book of insight walks down the centuries into our world with a word for the weary. It comes from a wise man nearing the end of his life, who wants to pass on wisdom gained through life's bitter and better experiences, to the generations yet to come.

Is That It?

Most of us are familiar with this restlessness—a longing, a vague feeling of discontent. Even if we are striving to live a godly life, we may feel unfulfilled. We ask, *What is the meaning of life?* And the answer seems to elude us.

Solomon asked the same questions. Although he was a man of great wealth and unsurpassed wisdom, he spent a lifetime searching for contentment, to finally realize that no relationship, no accomplishment, no experience can truly satisfy our souls. True happiness can be found in God alone. In the following chapters, I never want to minimize our deep human needs, but instead I will acknowledge them. We have a need for significance; for joy; for contentment; for love; for wisdom; for security; and for things to make sense. The collective heart cry takes many forms. Perhaps it is a longing for serenity: the tranquility of order, deep down in our souls. Sometimes it is a heart cry for a soul mate: a profound desire to matter to somebody who will love us. People of every creed, class, and color tell us they are just trying to find a little happiness!

The world seems to offer fulfillment of our needs but in reality, what the world offers is counterfeit. I invite you to walk with me through Ecclesiastes as we discover what it really means when we say that God alone is the answer, and that only in Him will we find the peace and satisfaction we crave.

Is it an easy path? No, this book doesn't pretend that it is. For some of our questions, we will not find answers this side of heaven—and that's certainly not easy to take! But this book from Solomon offers contemporary guidance for finding peace and contentment by living life in light of eternity.

Both Christians and non-Christians struggle to understand the point of our crazy, mixed up, materialistic world. We long for something so much deeper and truer than anything we find on earth. Too often, we respond to restlessness, loneliness and longing by trying to adjust our circumstances. We take our eyes off of Christ and run to the gods we create to prevent us from feeling broken and vulnerable.

Solomon addresses the universal heart cry for meaning and purpose. He poses the secular person's question—*What is the point of living, when death is inevitable?*—and answers it from a spiritual perspective. The wonderful little book of Ecclesiastes tells us that all of life is meaningless, hollow, futile and vain if it is not rightly related to God. When we live our "here and now" in the light of "there and then," God has promised rich experience here on earth, and a meaningful eternity where He will right all wrongs and make all things beautiful!

We will do well to listen to him and learn the most important lesson of all: we must find our reason for being in a meaningful relationship with God, fearing Him and keeping His commandments. That is the whole thing! Listen to the Teacher—your eternal destiny may depend on it.

CHAPTER 1

SEARCHING FOR SIGNIFICANCE

In a Put-Me-Down World

I, the Teacher, was king over Israel in Jerusalem. I devoted myself to study and to explore by wisdom all that is done under heaven. What a heavy burden God has laid on men! I have seen all the things that are done under the sun; all of them are meaningless, a chasing after the wind.

ECCLESIASTES 1:12-14

Have you found what you wanted in life? Or are you still searching?

Perhaps you have been looking in all the wrong places. You still feel empty and vaguely aware something isn't quite right. You wonder if your own life has any particular meaning. You are struggling to find significance in a world that just seems to diminish you. You are realizing that this life does little to affirm personal significance—it is indeed a put-me-down world.

Well, we are living here for this very reason: to discover purpose, meaning and significance. But as the writer of Ecclesiastes warns us, this lifetime is tragically transient. As he puts it: "Utterly meaningless! Everything is meaningless" (1:2). The Hebrew for "meaningless" is *hevel*, which means literally, vapor or mist. Some translations have it as "brief." Life is frustratingly short and amorphous. Christians, however, believe that God in His grace has given us enough precious moments to discover a spiritual reality that gives significance to our lives, however momentary they are.

I'm How Old?

Who has not woken on a birthday morning and thought, I'm *how* old? And I haven't done anything of real significance yet? At some point, all of us come to realize that life is brief. And yet strangely, we don't want to believe that *we* are brief. As the birthdays add up, we find it more and more difficult to believe we're really "that old" and that our lives are coming closer to the end. Even when you're old you don't really believe the person celebrating all these birthdays is you!

Coming out of church late one snowy Wisconsin night, I slipped and fell—and knocked myself out! My husband and one other man were the only people left in the parking lot when I came to. I could hear the other man on the phone to the hospital saying, "Please send an ambulance—an elderly lady has just fallen in the parking lot." As I lay there happily (though with a considerable headache ensuing), I managed to smile at my husband and say, "Isn't that amazing! Someone else has just fallen in the parking lot at exactly the same time!" It never occurred to me the young man was talking about me!

You may laugh at my denial, but you'll be there soon enough. Trust me.

The deep conviction that we can't be "this" old (which is usually defined as however old you are at the moment), reveals the relentless inner necessity we all share to live on . . . and on . . . and on. It's the same conviction that shouts in my spirit as I awaken to my birthday morning every year: *Surely the person having all these birthdays is not me!*

The human race struggles against the reality of bodies that are dying and minds that are confused. This is the work of sin and death—the result of the Fall. In fact, I'd be willing to guess that every person alive today struggles to some degree with the reality of death in the mind and in the body. Each day, we realize that we're breaking down, slowing up, losing our grip. Then, not knowing how else to respond to such dismal prospects, an irrepressible inner voice rises up, insisting that this just *isn't* the way things ought to be!

The irrepressible inner voice is right.

Somewhere in the depth of our souls, we know that there must have existed a very different plan for our lives than the reality we're experiencing. We were meant to live *on*. We were meant to exist *forever*. We were designed and created for so much more than what our earthbound lives can offer!

There's a Snake in Our Garden

As I travel the world I have found a universal heart-deep cry for answers to questions about life and death. What is the point of living life at such short notice for such a short time? Some inner voice tells us our very existence is important, so important it seems it should be considerably longer than it is.

For one thing, we know we are "fearfully and wonderfully made" (Psalm 139:14) and it would appear to be an inordinate waste of somebody's time to make us in such a blindingly brilliant fashion for such a brief encounter with life! Surely such creative exuberance and attention to miraculous detail could have—and would have—determined our body parts should never wear out.

It is an easy step from this premise to believe such a loving creative genius must have been horribly and nefariously sabotaged through some evil intent somewhere along the way. Yes, there is indeed a snake in our garden.

We believers call that snake Satan, and the incident—the evil interference—we call "the Fall." In a garden, underneath a tree, a man and woman's choice shortened God's intended timeline for our lives from eternity to three score years and ten. What should have been part of the eternal birthright of humankind, the ability to *live forever*, lay shattered on Eden's nursery floor. What would have been realized by innocence was lost. It *should have* been different.

This deeply conscious *should have* comes along at birth, seemingly packaged inside every baby's head. The insistent *should be* principle provokes us to think toward a possible solution. This, along with other spiritual stimuli, drives a person to search for answers to *the way things ought to be*. It's as if we're looking at a photo out of focus. We want to take out our cameras and take more pictures until a clear and correct image of how things *ought to be* is captured.

The Teacher in his writings tells us that God has "set eternity in the hearts of men" (3:11). That statement makes so much sense to me as I listen to people's searching questions. There is this spiritual drumbeat down in the soul that sends out a continuous message to the brain. It keeps popping up in our minds like an IM message on the computer, insisting we are eternal beings made by an eternal God, for eternal time in eternal places! To borrow a phrase from C. S. Lewis, there is something inside suggesting, "I was made for another world."[1]

In his book *The Great Divorce*, Lewis writes: "I believe, to be sure, that any man who reaches heaven will find . . . that the kernel of what he was really seeking even in his most depraved wishes will be there, beyond expectation, waiting for him in 'the High Countries.'"[2]

I believe in Lewis's "High Countries" and in the secret inner knowledge that there is something more, something we seek in this lifetime without even knowing what we're looking for. And I believe, with Lewis, that there is "somewhere to go" after death. There is Someone to meet who is greater than ourselves—and that leads me to believe there is something to accomplish for this Someone before we ever get to the somewhere! The soul is on a search. Your still, small, insistent voice is saying something valuable. Don't ignore it!

A Place of Spiritual Reality

The fact that we all seem to have this "heart cry" points me toward an inner certainty that, contrary to the voices of atheists and other non-Christians, another place somehow must exist. In fact, the Bible reveals details about life in these High Countries. It tells us that there is a road called "the way everlasting" that will lead you there (Psalm 139:24). I saw a billboard by the side of a freeway that said:

Will the road you're on get you to My place?
— GOD

It was really quite an arresting question as you drove along to the supermarket to buy some hamburger! I wondered what others thought about the sign. Where is "His place" anyway? And how do I know I'm on the right road to get there?

The Scriptures tell us that this "road" takes us to what "God has prepared for those who love him" (1 Corinthians 2:9). This is the "something more" that we're wondering about! The road takes us to the heavenly places of spiritual realities here on earth in this brief life—a relationship with God through Jesus Christ. And afterward, the road takes us to His house in the High Countries. This is the place that Jesus spoke of in the upper room when He promised the disciples that He was preparing a place for them—and for us (see John 14:1-4).

So our hearts cry out for more, and Scripture answers that "more" is available to us in this life and afterward, if we are on the right road. Since the need to "get there" is so universal, surely there must be many "right roads," don't you think? All roads lead to Rome? Or in other words—all religious paths lead to the same God?

But the answer to the heart cry is the sometimes-difficult truth, *there is only one road that will get you there.*

There is one road to heaven and Jesus said He would show us where it was and He would put us on it. "I am the way," He said (John 14:6). Jesus Christ is the road! Knowing God through Christ is the most important thing in the world. It is the only way to satisfy the deep yearnings we all have—for love, meaning, significance, peace, and all the other things our hearts cry out for.

"But Jill," I hear you say. "Surely that's not fair. What happens if people are born in a country where they have never seen a Bible or heard about Jesus? Surely God will let them in the front door of heaven if they were sincere and followed the only road they knew?"

No, that's not the way it works. Let me give you an illustration. Years ago I was trying to get to a meeting in a town quite distant from where I lived. I asked a friend who knew the area for directions. She gave me them saying, "Get on such and such a road and keep on it to the end. You will see a small service road with a hedge alongside it. Make sure you get on this narrow road."

I did the best I could. I turned when I saw the hedge, and I sincerely thought I was on the right road. Suddenly in my rear view mirror I saw lights. They didn't seem to be the lights of a car. They were sort of high up! To my horror I realized that I had—quite sincerely—gotten myself onto a tram track. My friend had been right: there was indeed a hedge on one side. There was also a hedge on the other! Once I was on this track, I couldn't get off!

There were actually two tracks side by side, and on the tracks next to me, I suddenly noticed a tram coming toward me from the other direction! I narrowly missed it, scratching the side of my vehicle on the hedge. Finally I came to a tram station, where a police car met me, siren whining. The people in the tram station were more than a little surprised to see me! The policeman was not only astonished, I'd say he was fairly well amazed. He told me I had broken the law and would have to pay a penalty. I tried to ask him which law I had broken, but he was not up for discussion. I told him I was sincere, had made an honest mistake, and didn't know there was a penalty for being on the tram track. It made no difference. I was on the wrong road, he said, and I would have to pay the price.

I might add that no matter how sincere I was, and how much I *wanted* to get to my meeting—that tram track was not going to get me there. It was not the correct road.

It's the same with a spiritual road—and in fact, so much more important than simply finding the right way to a meeting. One road will get you there, while many others won't. So let me ask you. Will the road you're on get you to His place? That's the question that should occupy our minds and employ our energies.

The Teacher finishes his book with the statement, "Fear God and keep his commandments, for this is the whole duty of man" (12:13). Finding the right road to the right place must be what we are about. The Bible explains how to get on the right road to the right place, and assures us the God of grace gives us time, though brief, to search it out. Our search for significance—meaning for our lives—will only yield satisfactory results if we are on this road.

WE ONLY HAVE TODAY

As if the fact that there is only one road isn't challenging enough, we must contend with the reality that we have limited time to find that road and walk it. As the Teacher introduces the reader to his won-derings, he warns us of his wanderings. He had drifted far from the right road and wasted much of his life in meaningless pursuits, and is haunted by his own foolishness. He warns us—you can't do yester-day again! You only have today! It is one of the themes of his entire book. Now old and gray, the Teacher writes for the next generation. He knows through bitter experience how horrifyingly possible it is to allow time to be crowded with anything and everything in the world, and never to get around to using these graciously given moments to look for God. Significance will only be found if we use life's fleeting minutes for seeking God's truth in our crazy, mixed-up world.

Solomon mourns his wasted years, willful apostasy and lost opportunities. He advises, "Remember your Creator in the days of your youth" (12:1) before, he implies, you are too old to remember anything anymore! This reminds me of a little rhyme that says:

My glasses come in handy, my hearing aid is fine

My false teeth are just dandy, but I sure do miss my mind!

We joke about our advancing years but laughter will not stop the birthdays coming like telephone poles along the side of the highway. And the older we get, the more set we become, not only in our ways, but in our willingness to think new thoughts, dream new dreams and question our presuppositions.

"Remember him" urges the Teacher, "before the silver cord is severed, or the golden bowl is broken; before the pitcher is shattered at the spring, or the wheel broken at the well, and the dust returns to the ground it came from, and the spirit returns to God who gave it" (12:6-7). Remember Him before it is too late! Remember Him—because everything else is futile, vain, empty.

"'Meaningless! Meaningless!'" says the Teacher. 'Everything is meaningless!'" (12:8). Various translations render the word in Ecclesiastes 12:8 as "brief" or "futile" or "vanity." Some may argue that the brevity of life can make it appear meaningless when you compare it to eternity, but the Teacher argues that because of life's brevity there is all the more reason to wrestle with the meaningless-ness of empty pursuits. We must not waste these precious moments. There is an urgency about it, yet our fallenness invites us to come and play—and it shouts louder than the voice of conscience.

Qoheleth's little book is full of examples of human fallenness —the author's and our own. Even in our willful mind-blindness, we, like the Teacher, know that things are out of sync. But we join the crowd out of sync—and sink! We know the truth but live in the lie. We silence the "should" of conscience and get on with life as it is offered in "Snake Land."

WE LIVE IN A FALLEN WORLD

Most people—even non-believers—don't doubt the theory of a fallen race. All we have to do is read the obituaries or go to a funeral, pick up a newspaper, turn on the TV, watch one more marriage fall apart, or read about oppression, injustice, rape, or terrorism. The theory is underlined when we hold a malformed baby in our arms, visit a prison, suffer betrayal, or find ourselves breaking a promise or suffering sexual abuse.

Try being a grandparent sitting in a courtroom watching a stranger divide up your grandchildren. Something inside you screams: Surely God had something so very different in mind when He set the lonely in families (see Psalm 68:6). This is not the way things *ought* to be! This state of affairs breaks the heart of God.

The harsh realities of life are the reason many try to hide from the harsh realities of life! It is often in order to cope that we turn to pleasure, noise, self-gratification, drink or drugs. It is not always fun for fun's sake that takes us down that pleasure road, but rather tragedy and trauma. But the Teacher, knowing this, tells us that it's better to go to a funeral than a party — a funeral, after all, wonderfully focuses the attention on what really matters (see 7:2). The hard things in life can be the means of searching a little harder for answers to our heart quest. In the end, pleasure can also turn us to God — for having tried everything in Pleasure Land, we will come up empty-handed.

That we are meant to search out the God of heaven is indicated to thinking people by the fact that every child born into this world asks the "why" questions as soon as they can talk. They become self-conscious in a hurry and rush around our living rooms asking why they are called living rooms. They want answers, and they want them now!

At six years of age, sitting in a Liverpool bomb shelter during the Second World War, I wanted to know why someone was trying to kill me, my sister, and my mother. I didn't get any answers. Later, looking at an exhibition of Nazi camp paintings by a survivor, I wondered who these dreadfully abused Jewish people were. I had thought they were God's people. I thought these thoughts as quietly as I could in case God, who I knew had excellent hearing, was listening in. "Well," my thoughts continued (or it could have been the snake), "aren't you glad you're not one of God's people if that's how He looks after His own?"

What had gone so very wrong in the world? I wondered. What

was the point of it all? What was the reason for being alive, if all that made up my life was sitting in an underground dugout at the bottom of our garden waiting to be buried by a bomb? I would have given my right arm to have someone give me some answers to my six-year-old questions. In those days nobody, however young, could fail to ask questions about the shoulds and shouldn'ts, the oughts and ought nots.

WHO AM I? WHY AM I?

Many years later after coming to Christ, leaving the teaching profession and going into ministry, I was looking after Drew, our three-year-old grandson. I noticed he was running around the house announcing with great excitement, "I be cold, I be naked, and I be hungry!" One day to my amazement he said, "I be me!" He was discovering his "being." It has been my observation as a preschool teacher that it isn't long before the child is asking *"Why* do I be me?"

It is a small step from asking "Why am I?" for the child to start asking, "What am I here for, and what am I supposed to be doing?" In other words, is there any real significance in my existence? An innate sense of self-importance surfaces. "I am *being* for a reason, a reason that is important. I know it. So what is it?" The child has a suspicion that there is indeed a big reason for his existence that no one is telling him about. He begins to behave as if he is the most important person in the whole wide world.

We, of course, are delighted with the little imps being so clever and forward. As parents, we agree with them—they are the most important little people in the world! And yet we big grown-up kids can actually get through our entire lives and never have the answers. You can even get really old, about to step off the end into space, and not have a single idea about the purpose of your existence. The Teacher talks a lot about what a sad waste of a life that is. Imagine an epitaph on a gravestone that says, "Here lies John Smith, who lived his life on this earth without knowing why he entered it." How sad.

So what, after all, is the significance of being *me*?

Our significance is completely God-given. He has given each of us our purpose, our reason for existence. When I seek and find God, *His* significance gives me mine. When I learn to fear and obey Him, I have found the secret of living life on this little swinging planet. As the Teacher concludes, "Fear God and keep his commandments, for this is the whole duty of man" (12:13). This is the whole thing!

But when I was young, I didn't know this. It could be that like me, you have had no one to answer your questions. What is the *whole thing* really about? Living in so-called "Christian" England, it took me eighteen years to ask those questions out loud. In God's grace, I asked the right person at last. She gave me the right answers and I found the right reason for living.

Does Anyone Know About This?

I found such deep purpose and meaning and fulfillment in seeking Christ that I was compelled to ask the girl who led me to Him, "Does anyone else know about this?" She laughed, "Of course," she replied, "why do you ask?"

"You mean all those people sitting in church knew about this, and they never went out of their way to tell me?"

I have never recovered from the shock. How anyone who truly knows Christ can ever sleep more than four hours a night beats me. How can we who know the answers to the eternal *why* in people's hearts do anything other than continually share it with others? We must "go into all the world" and tell what we know. How can I watch people filling their lives with water when I own the wine cellar? How could I find the cure for cancer and keep the secret to myself? Not me! The fact that *we have the answers* is just too exciting, too important not to share.

This poem by Jason Lehman came to me through the mail a long time ago. It sums up the dilemma of the person who thinks the answer is just around the corner, or perhaps just behind their back, or even under their nose right now, but they can't seem to see it.

PRESENT TENSE

It was Spring, But it was Summer I wanted,
The warm days, And the great outdoors.
It was Summer, But it was Fall I wanted,
The colorful leaves, And the cool, dry air.
It was Fall, But it was Winter I wanted,
The beautiful snow, And the joy of the holiday season.
It was Winter, But it was Spring I wanted,
The warmth, and the blossoming of nature.
I was a child, But it was adulthood I wanted,
The freedom, And the respect.
I was 20, But it was 30 I wanted,
To be mature, And sophisticated.
I was middle-aged, But it was 20 I wanted,
The youth, And the free spirit.
I was retired, But it was middle age I wanted,
The presence of mind, Without limitations.
My life was over.
But I never got what I wanted.

How incredibly sad! We only have today—not yesterday, not tomorrow. If we don't appreciate it *right now*, we'll miss it! Today is where we'll find our significance. Let's not waste one more minute. As we continue our journey through the pages of Ecclesiastes with the Teacher, I pray you will find yourself. You could also find God!

FOR GROUP OR PERSONAL STUDY

Quietly MIND MANAGE these concepts:

1. Do you feel significant? Do you know why you are here? Have you found what you wanted? If someone asked you, "What on earth are you doing?" could you give them an answer? Have you even thought about it?
2. If you believe that a creative intelligent God made you for an intelligent purpose, have you found it out? Are you searching?
3. Will the road you're on get you to His place? Are you sure you have found the Way everlasting? You may want to pray Psalm 139:23-24:

> *Search me, O God, and know my heart;*
> *test me and know my anxious thoughts.*
> *See if there is any offensive way in me,*
> *and lead me in the way everlasting.*

Discussion or Journal

1. Would you say you have found the meaning of life? What is it?
2. Which parts of this chapter struck a chord and why?
3. Will the road you're on get you to His place? Are you sure?
4. Read Psalm 139:23-24 again, then rewrite it in your own words.

Pray for Yourself and Others

- That God would search your heart and reveal anything hindering your relationship with Him.
- That you would be on the right road.
- That God would reveal His significant purpose for your own life.
- That you would have the strength, courage and persistence to never stop seeking Him.

Carry Out

What is the most important concept you need to take from this chapter? Write it out in a sentence or two. Is there any specific action you need to take?

ONE

*No one has ever seen God, but God the One and Only, who is at the
Father's side, has made him known.*

JOHN 1:18

One life lived
And one chance given,
One road home
Only one way to heaven.
One God waiting
His Life to impart:
One opportunity
To have Him in my heart!

One dreadful moment
In Eden's misty dawn
One disobedience
As sin and death were born.
One promise made,
Of a child yet to be
One life given—
On one crooked tree.

One cry of agony
That spanned the human race
One ghastly moment
In One grace-filled space
God's "One and Only"
Who loved me to the end,
In one melting moment
He became my friend!

Jill Briscoe

CHAPTER 2

SEARCHING FOR SENSE

In a World Gone Mad

Then I turned my thoughts to consider wisdom,
and also madness and folly.

ECCLESIASTES 2:12

Practical down-to-earth "life skills" are in much demand. Wisdom, or *God-sense*, is a priceless commodity. Have you ever needed to know what to do or say? I'm sure you have! In this crazy world we often find ourselves in human dilemmas that need far more than our small human effort to solve. We need wisdom.

I'm not talking about world-shattering problems, either. Family rows need as much mature diplomacy as do tribal disputes or all-out wars around the planet! For example, have you ever faced a teenager asking if he can go with his friends for a bike ride or a jaunt in a car, to a movie or party, and not known what to say? When our family came to live in the USA, our children were eleven, nine, and seven. As they roared into their teenage years we were in a very different and, to me, frightening culture. I felt very unsure of myself. I would have known if it was safe to ride a bike through a park in the UK but I didn't know if it was safe in America. What is a mother to do when the kids learn to drive so early in the USA and want to go cruising around town? (They didn't even have access to a car until they were working in the UK.) I needed wisdom from on high! I needed God-sense. Looking back on the years of winging those "Help Lord, give me wisdom" prayers heavenward, I thank God for protection, correction, and direction. He gave me wisdom well beyond my years and experience. Not that I always got it right—ask my kids!

Have you had to face a spouse who you have just discovered has betrayed you? What do you say? Where on earth do you start? Have you needed to terminate an employee? Have you anguished over a move, a letter that must be written, a church squabble that needs to be resolved? And what about sorting out things after a death in the family? Where there's a will there's a quarrel, so they say. Whoever "they" are — they are so often right!

So where do we start learning these spiritual street smarts? In the spiritual realm. We can turn to the wisdom of Ecclesiastes in the Word of God. "And who is sufficient for these things?" (2 Corinthians 2:16, KJV). He is! For this we have Jesus, who *is* our wisdom.

To keep our heads and live lives of sanity in a world gone mad, we need the wisdom of Solomon. Wisdom is *spiritual intelligence*. It's being savvy about managing your life choices and behavior. It's deep knowledge that copes with your own fallenness, and learns how to relate to fallen people living alongside you in a fallen world. It's down-to-earth good advice. It's being part of working out difficult relationships and helping others to do the same. It is far more than human intelligence, people skills or a good education. It is the "know how" to know "when and what" to say or do in a complicated situation. Wisdom is given by the Spirit of God when we are converted to Christ and become a Christian. And God is faithful to keep on increasing our wisdom as we continue asking — and studying His Word.

START AT THE END TO FIND THE BEGINNING

We need to start at the end of the book of Ecclesiastes to understand what it is all about, since the style of this book is in a genre far removed from today's "fast food" type of literature! I drive my husband crazy because I always read the end of a book first. It sort of makes up my mind if it's worth my time reading it at all! Ecclesiastes makes a whole lot more sense when you go to the end to find out about the beginning.

It's at the end of chapter 12 that the whole thing is summed up. "Here is the conclusion of the matter: Fear God and keep his commandments, for this is the whole duty of man. For God will bring every deed into judgment, including every hidden thing whether it is good or evil" (verses 13-14).

Solomon concludes his work with a summary of the results of all his heart searching, experimenting and discovering. It has been hard work for Solomon. "I wanted to see what was worthwhile for men to do under heaven," he explains (2:3). It took a lot of his life to find the answers but at the end he came to a satisfactory conclusion: Keep His commandments. This is the meaning to our existence. It's the whole thing. *The Message* renders Ecclesiastes 12:13-14: "Fear God. Do what he tells you. And that's it." That's what? The reason we are here—the whole purpose of life in this place, in this time.

There is an old saying: Fear God and live as you like! It makes sense that if you live in the fear of God you will live as He likes you to live. This is the only certain pathway to extreme joy, to living a life that makes perfect sense. Ecclesiastes teaches us that the pathway to an exuberance of living is realized by those who live within the boundaries set by His love. Those limits are simple. We *don't* "do this" and we *do* "do that." *This* and *that* being the ten rules God wrote in His own handwriting on a couple of slabs of rock on a mountain on fire! We call them the Ten Commandments.

Man's wonderings and wanderings find their end in a relationship with our Maker, pleasing and serving Him. That's the whole thing! Wisdom is coming to that conclusion as soon as possible, in order not to live a wasted and frustrated life. It is the only path that makes sense of life on planet earth. It's God-sense. This advice comes to us from numerous places in the Word of God including from the wisest man who ever lived—King Solomon.

PASSING ALONG A HERITAGE

Solomon concludes his writings by addressing the next generation. Here we have a man wanting to pass on lessons he had learned the hard way and hopefully warn others of the results of disobedience. After a life lived without the fear of God, he exhorts his followers to "Remember your Creator in the days of your youth" (12:1). But how do you "remember your Creator" when you are having far too much fun? Today the younger generation asks, why can't life be all about *now* and all about *me*? Our society gives young people today a frightening freedom to live as they wish—but not a freedom to choose the consequences of their choices!

Solomon warns, "Be happy, young man, while you are young, and let your heart give you joy in the days of your youth. Follow the ways of your heart and whatever your eyes see, but know that for all these things God will bring you to judgment" (11: 9). In other words you can reckon on a reckoning! There *will* be an accounting.

Did you know that if God gifts you with youth it is to be lived as if there was no tomorrow with which to experiment? And if He gifts you with age it is to be lived having no regret for yesterday? Solomon soberly reminds his readers that God will indeed bring judgment to all of us.

How does the Judge of all mankind give us personal significance and value? Doesn't the judgment of God mean that those who have done us down will "get theirs?" Yes, but it also means we will "get ours"! There will be some who arrive at the Great Day with empty hands and years to regret, and others who will hear, "Well done, good and faithful servant" (Matthew 25:21) for the good and faithful service they have rendered.

We are to live our lives in the light of sure and certain judgment to come. For the life we live will surely be evaluated by a just Judge. There will be rewards and there will be punishments, since "man is destined to die once, and after that to face judgment" (Hebrews 9:27).

More important than wondering if they will get theirs is not only to realize we will get ours, but most importantly, He will get His! His what? "To him who sits on the throne and to the Lamb be praise and honor and glory and power, for ever and ever!" (Revelation 5:13). But until that great day, we who were made in His image are meant to reflect His character—one element of which is wisdom.

So the Teacher opens his heart of wisdom and talks about life skill gained through life experience, married to knowledge and fear of the Lord. With honesty, humility and literary genius, he invites us to grow a pace, discovering a spiritual intelligence transmitted through our personal relationship with our wise God, who gifts us with an understanding of how to develop godliness: living it out in a hurt and broken world.

Where, exactly, does wisdom begin? Proverbs 9:10 tells us, "The fear of the LORD is the beginning of wisdom, and knowledge of the Holy One is understanding." *You can't have wisdom without having God.* We are not born naturally wise! You and I need to live connected to Him and therefore connected to His wisdom if we are to live well and happily "under the sun." (A phrase Solomon uses, meaning life lived on the earth.)

THE DREAM OF A LIFETIME

So wisdom is found beyond the place where mere human knowledge exists. God gifted Solomon with human knowledge. As soon as he took power he knew his own limited intelligence wasn't enough for the huge task ahead. Called to fill his father's sandals, Solomon asked God for more.

It's all right to ask God for more. More wisdom, that is. More wisdom than you possess. Try it! Get on your knees and ask Him for wisdom for the problems that face you at work, or in a relationship that is so complex you don't know which way to turn. Ask Him, and find the spiritual intelligence—the God-sense—that is yours for the asking.

Solomon's request is impressive. God appears in a dream and tells him to ask for anything he wants. Now that's the dream of a lifetime!

If it had happened to me I wonder what I would have asked for. What would you? Solomon asked for wisdom beyond himself to govern "this great people Israel." God was pleased with his answer, and seeing he was sincere, said in essence: "You didn't ask for health and you didn't ask for wealth, so I will give you what you asked for—wisdom such as no man has had before you or will have after you. And I will also give you what you didn't ask for: health and wealth!" (see 1 Kings 3:10-13). *A wise man or woman asks God for God-sense.*

We may not be ruling an entire nation, but we need to be God-wise in raising kids, or helping the disadvantaged, or being a lifesaver to a young man or woman who is drowning in life's troubled seas. Knowing what can only be known with God's help is more precious than the finest of gold.

Wisdom searches for the divine way in everything. It asks God for the right things. The wise person asks because he knows he cannot figure it out for himself. James says, "If any of you lacks wisdom, he should ask God, who gives generously to all without finding fault, and it will be given to him" (1:5). So we need to acquire the wisdom that comes from the only wise God—the Father of our Lord Jesus Christ.

How does this transfer of wisdom happen in answer to our request? *First, make sure you have asked God to give you Christ by His Spirit.* The New Testament tells us Christ is our wisdom and He is given to us when we realize we need a Savior, friend and a confidant. "It is because of him [God] that you are in Christ Jesus, who has become for us wisdom from God" (1 Corinthians 1:30).

Next, it's a question of appropriating—using—the wisdom and "life skills" we have already received. We do this on a day-to-day basis. It is foolishness to try and figure out the riddle of life all by ourselves. Solomon agrees. He says, "I saw that wisdom is better than folly, just as light is better than darkness" (2:13). It took him a while to tell the difference, but he got there in the end.

It may seem silly to keep banging this drum. Who wouldn't want to be wise instead of foolish? You'd be surprised! In his book *Wisdom: The Forgotten Factor of Success,* Philip Baker talks about "the cultivation of stupidity."[1] I have been amazed, reading his words, how verses from Ecclesiastes match his thoughts—and this is not a Christian book! Following are Baker's seven keys to being unwise. Each one is followed by a verse from Ecclesiastes that I have added to underline his argument.

Un-Wisdom, or How to Cultivate Stupidity

1. *Don't think.*
   "The wise man has eyes in his head, while the fool walks in the darkness" (2:14).
2. *Never be serious.*
   "'Laughter,' I said, 'is foolish. And what does pleasure accomplish?'" (2:2)
3. *Do as you feel.*
   "I denied myself nothing my eyes desired; I refused my heart no pleasure" (2:10).
4. *Make stupid friends.*
   "As goods increase, so do those who consume them" (5:11).
5. *Learn nothing from experience.*
   "Better a poor but wise youth than an old but foolish king who no longer knows how to take warning" (4:13).
6. *Never change your mind.*
   "The heart of the wise inclines to the right, but the heart of the fool to the left. Even as he walks along the road, the fool lacks sense and shows everyone how stupid he is" (10:2-3).
7. *Criticize continually.*
   "Words from a wise man's mouth are gracious, but a fool is consumed by his own lips" (10:12). (The Teacher is talking about the ability we have to criticize things that we know nothing about.)

"Age" Plus the Spirit's Intelligence Equals Wisdom

So how do we acquire wisdom? We acquire it from God, through His Spirit, by His Word. We listen to the teachings of His representatives down here on earth, His wise men and women—especially His aging ones! The older we get and the more we get to know the Lord through His Spirit, the more He prompts us to speak or stay silent. If we seek the Lord's wisdom throughout our lives, then as we age, we will also grow wiser!

So age, added to experience and mixed with wisdom from on high, has a message our generation needs to hear, put into practice and pass on to their generations to come! And that's what I want to do.

I remember my thoughts turning to Ecclesiastes as I was writing a newsletter I sent out about celebrating a very big birthday—my seventieth! I had a lot of response from this letter which found its way into magazines and books. It hit a note. This showed me there are a lot of mature folk like me at this stage, who need to be busier than we have ever been in our lives, sharing God's Word as much as possible before we run out of time. Let me share my experience.

"OVERTIME"

My birthday was coming up. A rather significant one. There was nothing I could do to stop it happening! I could wring my hands or stamp my feet; pout or fume, pray for hours, even call an all night prayer meeting with sympathetic friends to stave it off—it would do no good. It would happen anyway. As Jesus said 2,000 years ago, "Who of you by worrying can add a single hour to his life?" (or subtract one!) (Matthew 6:27).

A few years ago I was speaking at a women's event and

my hostess had left me a basket of fruit in my room and a little note card with a greeting and a verse of Scripture. After reading the note and the verse I went to look in the mirror. Better get a better publicity picture, I thought! The verse was Psalm 71:18. It said: "Even when I am old and gray, do not forsake me, O God, till I declare your power to the next generation, your might to all who are to come."

After sitting on the edge of my bed and meditating on the idea, I realized this was more than a kind note from the committee wishing to encourage an aging warrior who looked a little the worse for wear. This was a word from God!

Carefully I read the verse again and noted the one that came before it. "Since my youth, O God, you have taught me, and to this day I declare your marvelous deeds." I remembered my youth and my conversion at college in the UK. The wonder of discovering Jesus—or rather of Jesus discovering me—flooded over me. Pictures danced in my mind—of my friends' shocked faces as I struggled to explain whose I was and whom I now served. My friends, most of whom found it impossible to reconcile the new Jill with the old familiar one, left me.

I thought about my rich heritage, having heard John Stott and C. S. Lewis (a professor at Cambridge the same period I attended college there). I thought of my amazing opportunity to attend the famous Keswick convention and listen to celebrated British preachers, and I played back the memories of being taken along to hear a young and vibrant Reverend Billy Graham preach at the renowned Harringay Crusade in London.

I thought of meeting and marrying the love of my life and fellow "declarer of His might and power" and how we left the business world and worked on staff at a youth mission together. I remembered roaming the streets of the UK and talking to kids who had never heard that Jesus was alive and had the power to change their lives as He had changed ours. And I thanked God all over again for my heritage of life and service. I thanked God for our three children, all busy declaring His power to their generation, with our grandchildren "in the blocks" getting ready to go. Not least, I thanked God for my British roots nurtured in American soil and the thirty-four learning, growing years at Elmbrook Church in Milwaukee, Wisconsin. Yes, the verses from Psalm 71 walked off the page and into my life that day years ago, making themselves at home. I took out my Bible and marked the place, so I would know where it was when I needed to remember it.

We—Stuart and I—had just been in countries where freedom for the church was curtailed. Sitting on the floor in a hot humid upper room with thirty pastors' wives, teaching the book of Philippians—the words of an aged man in a prison 2,000 years ago, restricted, yet declaring His power and might to the next generation of believers—I watched the careful attention and eager note taking. *Some of these women are younger than my own children*, I thought. In fact two of them were the age of our eldest grandchildren! These servants of Jesus were the next generation who would need to carry the torch to their children and grandchildren after them. They had no heritage like I had. They had few biblical helps, teachers or Bibles. Not one of the women had heard of the Beatles or for that matter Dr. Billy Graham! Things were just plain difficult. Yet there was so much joy and laughter. Worship was whispered, prayer intense; hunger for the Word of God evident. *Don't stop*, they asked me wordlessly after an hour and a half teaching session. What joy to be here! What privilege.

They knew about my birthday and had prepared a special cake. There was a little commotion downstairs and suddenly all the Bibles disappeared and a table appeared with my birthday cake on it decorated with my name. I was gently nudged into the center of a circle of women and a cake knife was put in my hand poised over the cake. My new friends gathered round and offered a hearty rendering of something that sounded vaguely like "Happy Birthday to You." This time the singing was at the top of their voices! Photos were taken. We celebrated. A little time passed and all was peaceful again and they said they were ready to finish Philippians 2. The cake disappeared—in case it was needed again. I will not soon forget this birthday!

The time came for me to return to the hotel, and a sweet young woman came to me shyly, struggling with her English. She said, "This last Sunday we honored our elderly people. And we gave them a verse of Scripture to encourage them. I want to encourage you too. Please come back someday and finish the lessons from Philippians. This verse is for you from the Lord."

I knew without looking where she had turned in her Bible, before she read in halting English, "Even when I am old and gray, do not forsake me, O God, till I declare your power to the next generation, your might to all who are to come." I cried. She cried. I promised her that if I could, I would come back another day.

We are told in the Word of God that our allotted lifespan is "threescore years and ten" (Psalm 90:10, KJV), so in one week's time I would have completed my allotted span and joined my husband in "Overtime"! Later, I asked a friend who is a soccer coach to tell me what he said to his players if they tied a game and found themselves in overtime. Without hesitation he said, *"If my players find themselves in overtime I tell them: 'Take risks and go for goal. Give it all you've got. Never give up!'"* I realized: that's what Stuart and I are doing. We are busier than ever, taking risks, going for the goal, giving it all we've got. We are sharing the wisdom God has so graciously granted us through the years. Hey, it's okay—in fact, it's a grand place to be! Hurry up and join us—the next generation is waiting!

(Jill Briscoe, June 2005)

Solomon would encourage us to seek wisdom and not folly. God-sense and not nonsense. And as we grow older and grow in our spiritual maturity, what a joy it is to pass on God's knowledge to the generations to come! As Solomon advises, let's not only seek wisdom from God, but share it with others.

FOR GROUP OR PERSONAL STUDY

Quietly MIND MANAGE these concepts:

1. "Then I turned my thoughts to consider wisdom, and also madness and folly" (Ecclesiastes 2:12). God-sense and nonsense. What was Solomon referring to with the words "wisdom" and "folly"? What are examples of each in your own life?

2. Read 1 Kings 3:3-15. What do you learn about wisdom from this passage? What do you learn about Solomon? About God? What do you learn for yourself?

3. The New Testament underlines this in James 1:5-6. Read this passage and take a few minutes to write it out and memorize it.

Discussion or Journal

1. What is another way we gain wisdom? Read David's words in Psalm 119:97-100.

> *Oh, how I love your law!*
> *I meditate on it all day long.*

> *Your commands make me wiser than my enemies,*
> *for they are ever with me.*

> *I have more insight than all my teachers,*
> *for I meditate on your statutes.*

> *I have more understanding than the elders,*
> *for I obey your precepts.*

2. Look back at page 43 and read about "un-wisdom" again, along with the corresponding verses from Ecclesiastes. Which aspect of un-wisdom strikes you, and why? Do any of them seem familiar?

3. Have you asked for wisdom from God yet? Can you see evidence that you are gaining wisdom from Him? If not, why?

Pray for Yourself and Others
- Ask God to give you wisdom and to guide you in studying His Word.
- Pray for the wisdom of others in your life, and ask that the Holy Spirit will help you and others interpret the Word and apply it to everyday life.
- Pray for any "older" and wiser Christians in your life, that they will have the strength and courage to pass along their wisdom to the younger generations.

Carry Out
What are you taking away from this chapter? How does it apply directly to your life? Make a list of three things.

SAGE WISDOM

*Now, O LORD my God, you have made your servant
king in place of my father David. But I am only a
little child and do not know how to carry out my
duties. . . . So give your servant a discerning heart to
govern your people and to distinguish between right
and wrong. For who is able to govern
this great people of yours?*

1 KINGS 3:7,9

Have you wondered what to say
Or what to do throughout the day?
When faced with children wild and strong
To give advice on right or wrong?
Do you like me need wisdoms' light
To pierce a dark dilemmas' night?

When Solomon had had a dream
And God had come or so it seemed,
And offered him a choice so rare
And told him not to dare despair,
When overwhelmed by life's demands
He gave his way into God's hands.

The Spirit's wisdom can be ours
When running out of human powers.
However young, however old
He'll give you words and you'll be bold
To find God's wisdom like the Sage,
To benefit your day and age!

Jill Briscoe

CHAPTER 3

SEARCHING FOR A SONG

In a World of Tears

He seldom reflects on the days of his life, because God keeps him occupied with gladness of heart.

ECCLESIASTES 5:20

How long is it since you've experienced a "heart song"? If your life is in confusion and you are crying inside, you probably won't be thinking of singing any songs. How can we sing a song when our hearts are breaking?

Well, the song may be in a minor key but I believe it is possible! When the Music Maker lives within our pain, the heart will not keep quiet. It is such a waste to spend the best years of our life sighing and crying, refusing to be comforted. Many of us settle down to wait until we are old and life sorts itself out (we hope) before we compose the praise that turns our mourning into dancing. But we don't need to wait—a song is possible right now.

SOMETIMES IN THE DARK — BUT NEVER AT A DISTANCE

Solomon had a few years left after returning to God to share with mankind his lessons of joy. Having lived as if God was absent from His universe and experiencing the heartache and misery of that approach, he came to understand that the person who marginalizes God is a miserable person indeed. No one wants to be around them—while the joyful person has friends galore.

What does life and death hold for a person with no use for the joyful God? What joy can be found for the person who talks as if he knows God but ignores Him and does not invite Him into his problems and his pain—a person who has marginalized God? Sometimes we speak noisily about God's presence, while secretly believing He is in fact absent. If this is how we live, then life and death are miserable events—the sooner over, the better!

Do you secretly think of Him as being absent? I remember a particularly black time of my life when nothing made sense. It seemed God had left my personal world to attend to more important things. He was surely absent! I had nothing to sing about though I continued preaching and teaching and telling people God was near. But I wondered.

Then I came across an old missionary book from at least a century ago, and in it I read that God sometimes hides Himself, but that doesn't mean He is absent. He is sometimes hidden in the dark, but He is never at a distance. He is always right here, whether we sense Him or not.

Did I believe He was present or absent? Was He nearer than breathing, closer than hands and feet? Or was He so busy organizing His stars into galaxies that He had no time to attend to my sad, sad heart? I had a choice.

I chose to believe He never absented Himself from His people. "Emmanuel" means *God with us*. Since I was one of His people, that meant me!

Only when we have faith in what the Bible says about Him, and stop pushing Him out to the circumference of our lives, can we find peace of mind, joy of spirit, and answers to our deep heart cry. If you marginalize God, your life may be fun for a little while, but will get old in a hurry. The scary thing is, if you marginalize God, one day He will marginalize you! In fact, He will do more than push you to the margins of heaven. He will tell you that you don't belong there at all. Then tears will flow forever. But once God has forgiven you for Christ's sake you will live with Him forever, and will have found the reason for living and dying. You will have a song in your heart.

LIVING FOR SOMETHING DEFINITE

Søren Kierkegaard's philosophy and writings have been summed up as the search for the single "idea for which I am willing to live and die."[1] The problem is that so many people have no "definite" aim or goal in their lives, no "idea" important enough to live and die for. Fyodor Dostoevsky wrote, "The secret of man's being is not only to live . . . but to live for something definite."[2] A man who loses his hope for a meaningful existence will soon find himself realizing, *I have no defining goal in my life, and what's more, no one with whom to talk about it! My universe has become silent as I turn away from God.*

The soul asks whether there is anyone home in the universe who cares a dime about what happens on this planet, even if the God of the universe did make it in some bygone age. Is there anyone out there to talk to? For the man who believes that there is no one home—no one there at the end of the journey—no one to explain what was it all about when we get to the end—that man has no alternative but to say with Solomon: "Meaningless, meaningless, all is meaningless!" Who is going to compose a song about that?

When I was a child, I remember one particular night when I was huddled in a bomb shelter. When the "all clear" sounded, we scrambled out hoping that the raid was over and we could go back to sleep in a bed for a change. I looked up at the sky. It was still night and all the stars were out. In my small mind, the stars looked like holes in heaven and all the light was shining through!

"It must be wonderful to be able to leave all the lights on in heaven," I thought. In our house we had to have the curtains drawn and all our windows shaded in black in case a chink of light showed through and the enemy dropped a bomb on us. What a happy and joyful thing to live in the light of all the glory of heaven! I remember thinking in my six-year-old mind, "Is anyone home in Heaven's House? Hello—is anyone there?" I wondered if God had indeed abandoned His heaven and moved to some far corner of some other world and left us alone. And if He was still home, did He see us? Did it bother Him to watch us killing each other? Was He indifferent to our woes and our wars and our worries and our tears?

Of course if He was present and not absent, I had a bigger problem than if He *had* moved house! What sort of a God could ignore the frantic cries of a child waiting to be buried by a bomb in an air-raid shelter? It didn't make sense if He was there — and it didn't make sense if He wasn't. Even looking back, I realize that my young mind was asking a good question! It would be quite a few more years before I had the answer to this.

CHASING THE WIND

Solomon concluded that trying, apart from God, to find answers to life's big questions was like "chasing the wind." He could find nothing that made sense of life or death — not pleasure, not work, not human wisdom. And how could anyone find joy in that? How can you have a song in your heart when there is no point to living? How futile to have lived and never to have known the key for living. What a waste to die without having enjoyed life or known what it was all about because you spent the whole time chasing elusive ideas about the point of it all.

After college I taught in the British school system. I used to take my turn on playground duty and watch the kids as they played. The windy days were the most fun. The small children would play a game they called "Who can catch the wind?" I noticed the game would be fun for a minute but would soon lose its attraction. It seemed as if the wind was having fun at their expense. The laughter would stop and the children would move on to more meaningful play.

Albert Camus, the French philosopher, is said to have thought of life as either absurd or simply a bad joke. And as we have seen, even the Teacher characterized life as brief—a vapor, a mist. If life is really a joke, then we have such a brief time to laugh at it! Life under the sun, he says, is boring, frustrating and meaningless.

The Daily Round and Round

In chapter 1 of Ecclesiastes the Teacher looks at the natural world and observes there is a pattern and a rhythm to its life. "The sun rises and the sun sets" (1:5). The wind blows always in the same direction, the streams flow into the sea—and Solomon finds it all meaningless! "So what?" he seems to say. What does that have to do with my life?

What's more, "there is nothing new under the sun" (1:9). The whole thing seems so boring, "wearisome" he calls it. It's the "same old, same old" as our teenagers would say. The daily "round and round" never seems to get "around" to doing anything significant! What is the point of the rivers running to all the same places all the time? Why do the winds have such a predictable pattern? Nothing ever changes. And that's a cardinal sin if you are young these days! Predictability is boring.

If there is one word that teenagers use as an indictment on life in general, it's the word "boring." It is the worst adult sin to bore them out of their skull (and so easy to do). But for those who have not met the Creator God and had their eyes opened to the wonders of His purposeful purposes and ordered blessings for us, then even the intricate work of God in heaven will appear to be boring.

If the daily round and round is not seen through eyes of faith, then, "What has been will be again. What has been done will be done again; there is nothing new under the sun. Is there anything of which one can say 'Look, this is something new'?" (1:9-10). Everything is so weary and tiresome here on earth! No matter how much we see, we are never satisfied. No matter how much we hear we are not content. That's how things look when we are separate from God.

And it is not only the environment that seems to have no pur-pose or meaning, "generations come and generations go, but the earth never changes" (1:4, NLT). Even people have no significance! History merely repeats itself; it has all been done before.

So Solomon says, "I devoted myself to search for understand-ing and to explore by wisdom everything being done under heaven. I soon discovered that God has dealt a tragic existence to the human race" (1:13, NLT).

EARTH'S CRAMMED WITH HEAVEN

But of course, it depends "how" you are looking at nature and at life's cycle. One of my husband's favorite quotes is from the poet Elizabeth Barrett Browning:

> *Earth's crammed with heaven,*
> *And every common bush afire with God:*
> *But only he who sees, takes off his shoes,*
> *The rest sit round it, and pluck blackberries . . .* [3]

I think also of some lines from a childhood hymn:

> *All good gifts around us are sent by heaven above:*
> *So thank the Lord, oh thank the Lord for all His love.*
> *He gave us eyes to see them, and lips that we might tell*
> *How great is God our Father who doeth all things well!* [4]

See the difference between God-seekers and self-seekers? Qoheleth reminds us that the one who has been introduced to the Ruler and Maker of it all, the one who is searching in all the right places, sees that "The heavens declare the glory of God; the skies proclaim the work of his hands" (Psalm 19:1). The Bible tells us there is enough evidence about the Creator in the things He has made to convince us all there is some pattern or plan—and it is a marvelous one. How sad to observe the order and rhythms of nature, and miss the glory of God!

THE INVISIBLE THINGS OF GOD

Years ago after the war my father took the family to France and Switzerland for a holiday. There were few hotels open so we found ourselves in the Alps with nowhere to sleep but the car. It was pretty uncomfortable and early in the morning I slipped outside, sat on a rock, and watched the day dawn.

Coming from a family that didn't attend church, I suddenly found myself in a cathedral! I was fourteen years of age and dumbstruck at the "finger work" of God. A strange thing happened. Instead of saying to myself, "How incredible is nature—I will become a nature lover!" I said, "How incredible is God, I will become a God-lover!" I ran to the car, got a pencil and piece of paper and scribbled out my first bit of poetry.

> *The day dawned softly filling me with awe:*
> *It seems the other side of heaven's door.*
> *That God forgives man's sin to me is plain*
> *Today in spite of sin*
> *The sun did rise again!*

Not good syntax—but pretty good theology, though I did not know it.

What was happening was described in a Bible I hadn't read. In Romans chapter 1, the apostle Paul tells us that through the things God has made, we "can clearly see his invisible qualities—his eternal power and divine nature" (verse 20, NLT). As I watched the sun rise, I was watching the grace of God give us wretched men and women one more day to figure it out, repent of our sin and come home. In spite of the mayhem, the killing, the sorrow and sadness in my world, the sun had risen again! Joy!

I knew without a shadow of a doubt that the God of Eternity had set me down on that rock and written out the gospel of grace for me in an incredible sunrise. Another day was mine—another chance to open my eyes to Him, a brand new chance to fear Him and obey His commandments. I didn't know the Bible yet, but somehow I knew: This was *The Whole Thing!*

"Somebody" had put eternity in my heart and Somebody had given me the gift of time—however brief—to realize it. Somebody whispered to my soul that I was made for another world. I caught an inkling that although I live my life this side of the front door of Forever, somehow I can know that Somebody is home in the universe and is waiting for me.

He was waiting to ask me, *What on earth were you doing?* Would I answer, "I was chasing the wind"? Would I hear Him say, "That is not exactly what I had in mind for you"? Or would I answer Him, "Lord God, as best I knew how, I feared You and kept Your commandments, for that is the reason You created and redeemed me, and that is my chief end and highest Joy!" That day sitting on the rock was my first step toward finding the right answer—living with a song in my heart, though the world remained in turmoil around me.

LIFE IN A BOWL OF CHERRIES — OR LIFE IN THE PITS?

It was Erma Bombeck, the comedienne, who wrote a book titled, *If Life Is a Bowl of Cherries, What Am I Doing in the Pits?* There is a certain rhythm to life lived here, life after the Fall, as Qoheleth explains. Sometimes it is a bowl of cherries, and sometimes it is the pits. That's life under the sun!

For some, it's the pits at the moment. Nothing is going right. There is just one bad thing happening after another. Perhaps you are in a pain pit, or a pressure pit. Maybe you are in a parent pit, or a pity pit. It could even be a poverty pit. As far as you are concerned, life under the sun is "the pits"!

Life "in the Son," on the other hand, can be like living in a bowl of cherries. Life "under the sun" takes on a whole new meaning when you experience life "in the Son." If you get to know Christ, even if you are in the pits, the unacceptable becomes acceptable. The thorn in the flesh, as the apostle Paul puts it, is tolerated and even welcomed. Paul found himself as happy with it as without it—because Christ gave him strength. I'm not saying you won't have problems. In fact you will probably have a whole new set! But when you live in a deep and growing relationship with Christ, you live well with them. You can live contentedly in your problems—and above them.

So what is it for you? Are you living in relationship with the living God, through Christ? Life not simply "under the sun" but "in the Son"? If you are, you will know. He comes to our pits and offers us outrageous joy and a peace that passes understanding. He gives us an inner settled assurance that tells us that one day, He will make everything beautiful in its time (see Ecclesiastes 3:11). Not today, perhaps not tomorrow, but one day! Such God-given assurance and serenity beggars the mind! This is indeed what it means to have a song in your heart.

FINDING JOY IN THE ORDINARY

I once heard someone say, "Peace is faith resting: joy is faith dancing!" Peace and joy go together. Is there joy in the book of Ecclesiastes? I must admit, when I first read it I thought it was all fatalistic material, all doom and gloom. Well there is plenty of that, but oh, the joy I found in all sorts of unexpected places.

First, I saw that the Teacher talks about finding joy in the ordinary things of life. "Then I realized that it is good and proper for a man to eat and drink, and to find satisfaction in his toilsome labor under the sun during the few days of life God has given him—for this is his lot" (5:18). There is nothing quite so ordinary as food and drink and a job! They are meant to provide us satisfaction, yet they seem to be the things most grumbled about. The secret is right here in the next verse: "Moreover, when God gives any man wealth and possessions, and enables him to enjoy them, to accept his lot and be happy in his work—this is a gift of God" (5:19). Do you see it? These ordinary things are gifts from the Provider, and the joy we can find in them is also a gift! It is God who enables us to enjoy our gifts. *The enjoyment of all these things is a gift in itself!*

So according to Qoheleth, finding joy and serenity of heart and mind—contentment with your lot in life, whatever it is—is a gift. The person who asks God to give him or her the ability to accept their lot and enjoy the simple things in life doesn't worry about the past because it is forgiven. They need not worry about the present because it is carried by a God with broad shoulders, and the future is in His hands as well! In fact, "He seldom reflects on the days of his life, because God keeps him occupied with gladness of heart" (5:20). In other words it's useless to brood over food or drink or jobs—or how long we might live. Better to find the joy in the ordinary, and go through life with a song in your heart. It's a choice!

So what is occupying your heart and mind right now? Are you content with your lot, or always comparing your lot in life with that of others? Are you forever worrying about what you will eat, drink or wear? Do you know it is possible to be occupied instead with "gladness of heart"? As *The Message* puts it, "Yes, we should make the most of what God gives, both the bounty and the capacity to enjoy it, accepting what's given and delighting in the work. It's God's gift! God deals out joy in the present, the now" (5:19-20). The gift of gladness of heart is wrapped up with the gift of God in Christ. Jesus is joy—joy is Jesus, and with the gift of the Son, life "under the sun" becomes a whole new thing!

OCCUPIED WITH JESUS' JOY

First and foremost, joy is to be found in His ever-present presence. "You have made known to me the path of life; you will fill me with joy in your presence, with eternal pleasures at your right hand" (Psalm 16:11).

Joy has to do with the conscious presence of God. God keeps such a man or woman occupied with gladness of heart. The goal is to be engaged in the inner recesses of your life with God Himself. Not God and you, or God and riches, or God and health. Not God and kids, or God and no kids. Not God and shelter or food. Not God and marriage, God and a new car or a new career. God's presence gives a new dimension to all good things which Ecclesiastes teaches are *all* God's gifts. God's presence is itself the greatest gift.

My mother-in-law's favorite hymn was a beautiful song that echoed her experience after coming to Christ.

> *Heaven above is softer blue*
> *Earth around is sweeter green,*
> *Something lives in every hue*
> *Christ less eyes have never seen.*
> *Birds with gladder songs o'er flow*
> *Flowers with deeper beauties shine*
> *Since I know as now I know,*
> *I am His and He is mine!* [5]

LIFE UNDER THE SUN

Once you experience life under the sun "in the Son," the good things are graced with His presence, and look quite different. Even the bad things graced with His presence can be seen in a new light. The Son makes us His and changes our whole outlook on trials and trouble, joys and delights. When God in grace gives us Christ to live in us by His Spirit, we find our hearts occupied with Him, reveling in His presence in a place no trouble can intrude—in the inner halls of our heart! The grace of God gives us strength and spiritual riches; the joy of salvation and the power to tell the world about it. Thank God for His grace! I wrote this poem one day when I was overwhelmed by the grace of God.

GRACE GAVE ME CHRIST

Dust am I, yet dust dignified with Divinity
Finite am I, yet graced to live in infinity;
Weak am I, yet strengthened in all my extremity
Grace gave me Christ!

Poor am I, but rich beyond expectation
Humble my lot, yet royal are all my relations!
Accepted am I, without putting me on probation,
God gave me Christ.

So I revel in God and I celebrate living
In the joy of salvation, and a God who keeps giving:
All the power that I need to tell worlds of His dying:
Grace gave me Christ.

While in prison Paul told us to rejoice in the Lord. We can do that whatever our circumstances. As *The Message* renders Philippians 4:4, "Celebrate God all day, every day. I mean, revel in him!"

So we can learn to revel, or enjoy Him. Not Him *and* friends, not even Him *and* freedom. Not Him and anyone or anything. I call this "Jesus joy." It is the joy He promised to all who are Jesus Lovers and Glory givers!

> *Joy is Jesus*
> *God in Galilean clothes*
> *Making my heart smile.*

When God came to earth in Christ; when He walked in our fields, and ate at our tables; when He wore our clothes, and went to our weddings and cried at our funerals; when He visited our pits and our bowls of cherries—He wanted us to know His joy. The cry of the human heart is for happiness. Our hearts are crying when they know they should be laughing. They are in turmoil and they know they should be at peace. Something is very wrong.

Jesus wanted us to know serenity despite heartache caused by life under the sun. Joy that flows from a heart untroubled by the troubles of life was intended to be a characteristic of His people. So one day He gathered His disciples around Him and said to them, "Ask and you will receive, and your joy will be complete" (John 16:24). Then He prayed to His Father that "they" (the disciples) "may have the full measure of *my joy* within them" (John 17:13, italics mine).

Jesus also said, "My peace I give you. I do not give to you as the world gives" (John 14:27). He gives peace as only He can give it! So when you can't praise Him for what He allows, praise Him for who He is, "in" what He allows. Receive His joy and peace. Often we think of prayer as giving. We give God information. We tell God all about it. (Although of course, He knows more about it than we do already!) Or we think of prayer as "asking"—reciting our shopping list for God. We need to learn to enter the presence of the Lord to *receive* as well.

Usually we rush into God's presence and talk our heads off. We have limited time and we want to make sure we have our say. This leaves little time for God to respond! We finish praying and move on with our day—without allowing Him to give us something. Maybe He wanted to show us a word of encouragement in the Scriptures, or to bring to mind a person who might help us with a problem. Or perhaps just to settle our frantic spirits and give us tranquility. God is left with His blessings in His hands as He watches us rush away and resume our activities. God always has something for us. Make sure you take the time to receive it.

DANCE TO THE BEAT OF HIS HEART

At the worst point of the initial bombings in Israel as the First Intifada (the Palestinian uprising) began in the late 1980s, Stuart and I were in a hotel in Jerusalem. One bomb exploded outside our hotel at the bus stop, killing many innocent people. That night we went downtown (cautiously) to a meeting. Never have I been surprised by so much Jesus-joy! A choir had come from Britain to pray for the church in Israel in their trouble. The people of Jerusalem who loved the Lord—Jew and Arab alike—gathered to add their voices, their praise and their prayers. They could not praise Him for what He had allowed to happen, but they could praise Him for who He was in the midst of pain and suffering. And they did.

Things look and feel different when we take the time to praise Him. Praise focuses our attention away from us. This always helps, since our constant need is to escape from the tyranny of self. One way is to concentrate heavenward. That is where worship begins. Praise can be musical, or spoken words, or even silent thoughts. Praise in the midst of even the worst turmoil can set your soul a-dancing!

The London Christian choir had brought a new hymn with them, and I will never forget singing it in the large gathering with such joy around me I could hardly stand it. These brothers' and sisters' hearts were dancing. Joy is to be found when we find Jesus Christ. As our heart-search ends in His arms, we dance to the beat of His heart. *Joy in trouble; joy in darkness; even joy when bus bombs are going off.* Jesus promised: our joy is His joy—realized. Here is a bit of what we sang that day:

TEACH ME TO DANCE[6]

Teach me to dance to the beat of your heart
Teach me to move in the power of your Spirit
Teach me to walk in the light of your presence
Teach me to dance to the beat of your heart.
Teach me to love with your heart of compassion
Teach me to trust in the word of your promise
Teach me to hope in the day of your coming
Teach me to dance to the beat of your heart.

You wrote the rhythm of life
Created heaven and earth
In you is joy without measure.
So like a child in your sight I dance to see your delight
For I was made for your pleasure.

(Graham Kendrick and Steve Thompson)

Let me ask you a question. How much peace and joy are you experiencing? What does it take to make you happy? Are you restless, bored, frightened and apprehensive all the time? How is life under the sun? Are you living in the Son? God can give you a song in a world of tears!

FOR GROUP OR PERSONAL STUDY

Quietly MIND MANAGE these concepts:

1. Are you bored by the mundane daily round? Or do you find joy in the ordinary things of life? What about your kids—do you find joy in them? (Be honest with yourself!) Read Ecclesiastes, chapter 1. Can you relate to Solomon's assessment of everything being "meaningless"?

2. Joy and serenity are the birthright of those who know and love God. Read Ecclesiastes 5:18-20. Paraphrase this section, related to your own life. Ponder. Are you receiving the gift of God's joy?

3. Think of a time in your life when joy has eluded you, and another when you felt God's amazing joy even though circumstances were difficult. Are you able to identify what made the difference?

Discussion or Journal

1. All of human existence when lived apart from God is frustrating and unsatisfactory. True or false?

2. All pleasure and the material things of life when sought for their own sake bring nothing but unhappiness and disappointment! True or false?

3. To experience spiritual exuberance—for your soul to "dance to the beat of His heart"—you need to personally know God. True or false?

Pray for Yourself and Others

- Ask God to give you the joy of His presence, regardless of the circumstances.
- Pray for your family, that they would have a song in their heart that can only come from the Music Maker.

- Pray for missionaries around the world, that they would not be overcome with frustration or impatience, but that they would have God's joy in their work.
- In your prayer time, sit in silence and receive the things God wants to give you.

Carry Out

What one thing do you have to sing about from the "processing" part of this study that you will "carry out" with you? Find one person to share that with this week.

CHASING THE WIND

I have seen all the things that are done under the sun;
all of them are meaningless, a chasing after the wind.

ECCLESIASTES 1:14

I'm Chasing the wind
And I'm empty inside:
Bored with life's boredom
With a faith that has died:
I can't seem to see You
In the things that You've made
Hopeless and helpless
I'm oh so afraid!

"Let joy in My presence,
Make your soul smile,
Dance to My heartbeat
As I make life worthwhile.
When pleasures entice you
For their own selfish ends
Leaving you hungry
Turn to Me and depend!"

Spiritual exuberance is ours for the asking
Strength and the gifting is given for the tasking,
Fear not tomorrow
Take strength from His hand
Then sing Him a song
As you live what He's planned!

Jill Briscoe
April 2006

CHAPTER 4

SEARCHING FOR SATISFACTION

In a Sex-Saturated World

> *I thought in my heart, "Come now, I will test you with pleasure to find out what is good." But that also proved to be meaningless.*
>
> ECCLESIASTES 2:1

We live in a sex-saturated culture. We get the impression from the media, films, music and books that you can't be happy and fulfilled without sex. Of course, this obsession extends to all the other things people pursue purely for their own stimulation—money, fame, drug and alcohol-induced "highs," status cars and a life of luxury. With the presupposition of the value of these pursuits comes the obvious premise that the "here and now" must be all-important. I have even had a conversation with a teenager who said something to the effect of, "Sex is the most important thing in life, and we need to enjoy as much as possible now—since even Jesus said there's no sex in heaven!" I presumed she was thinking of the Lord's remarks to the Pharisees that in heaven there is no marriage. But her remarks made me sad—and highlighted the pervasiveness of this idea in our culture.

ANY JOY DIVORCED FROM THE ETERNAL GOD CANNOT LAST

Life is brief and eternity is long, which leads me to believe that the physical joys we know now are temporary, and a whole lot less significant than spiritual joys. We know that God has put eternity in the hearts of men. The human race is born with a secret conviction that we are made to live in another dimension forever. Therefore, nothing but some eternal element can satisfy the thirsty soul. The Bible says that the soul is the most important part of us. I am not implying that the body is unimportant, but it is not, as our culture would have us believe, the *most* important! I believe that when people spend their lives in pursuit of self-indulgent pleasures, they are really trying to satisfy the hunger in their soul for the eternal. But surely they are looking in all the wrong places!

As the normal rhythm of life continues—living and dying, working and resting, marrying and burying, in joy and sorrow, through good times and bad—that insistent little voice troubles our souls. "Is this all there is?" it asks. And if the answer is yes, then there is nothing but fleeting joy to be found on earth and we had better make the most of it. In that case, the message of the sex-saturated culture must be correct! Physical pleasures would be all-important if all that mattered was the "here and now."

But the believer in Jesus has a secret. *Any joy divorced from the eternal God cannot last.* There is eternal joy only in a living relationship with Him.

The problem is exacerbated by an enemy. A terrible enemy who wants to prevent us ever hearing the insistent secret call of God to a relationship with Him that will fulfill us. He provides substitutes to distract us. The devil is a master of illusion; *everything you need is here and now,* he insists. *Have an apple—a nice juicy worldly apple—I'll gladly help you climb the forbidden tree and pick it! Then you and I will enjoy it together.* That battle ensues everyday. We see it in our money-grabbing greed culture, and our pleasure-oriented, sex-saturated world!

SINCE ADAM WAS A LAD

The devil's devices haven't changed. He has been at it since "Adam was a lad"! He wants to tempt us to believe we are gods: masters of our own destiny, controller of the times and seasons, provider of our own needs and wants, even sustainer of our own lives!

"Everything you need to be fully human and happy is here and now," he whispers. There is no forever. So if this is all there is—go for it! Control your destiny on earth and don't worry about the future. He badly wants us to practice "god-man-ship" of our own lives, which is "self-ship." Or you might call it "self-liness" as opposed to true "godliness." He is eager for us to become obsessed by the personal pronoun. It's an illusion, of course, that this is where meaning and happiness lie. But it's seductive. "Get what you want and you'll want what you get" just isn't true.

Solomon knew better than to adopt this philosophy, but there was a time in his life when he grew lax in his spiritual disciplines and bought into the lie. He found the lifestyle of endless hedonistic pleasures to be empty and futile. He said, "I denied myself nothing my eyes desired" (2:10). In other words, he had every single earthly thing he ever wanted—riches, beautiful homes, all the sex he could handle, and the most marvelous food and drink available at that time. Yet he found no lasting fulfillment—only momentary gratification. What was his conclusion? "So I hated life . . . all of it is meaningless, a chasing after the wind" (2:17). And he said this even after his romp with over a thousand women! He still chased the wind because it was never enough, and he could never find contentment in his earthly pursuits. He had become obsessed with the chase and couldn't seem to turn himself around. He needed help from above.

A Must-Have Culture

We suffer from a "getting" obsession fed by a "must have" culture. Look at the advertisements. The advertisers play to the "greed need" in us. *Eden's appetite*, I call it. To see it . . . is to want it. To want it . . . is to *have* to have it. Solomon had the means to get it and as he testifies, "I never said no to myself" (2:10, MSG). Do you know anyone who never says "no" to himself or herself? I do! Me, for one! At least that's how "the old me" would like to have it—and the old me tries to have her way far too often.

Solomon indulged himself with wine, women, and song—but

his wine only chloroformed his conscience, his women promised more than they delivered, and he ended up singing a very sad song. "I find more bitter than death the woman who is a snare, whose heart is a trap and whose hands are chains," he laments (7:26). He grieves that he could not find "one upright woman" (7:28). He had all the women he wanted and also the means to possess every object he desired in his world. Still, he was not fulfilled.

Our own "must have" culture isn't only obsessed with getting everything we crave, it is obsessed with "being" the sort of person we each want to be. I must "be" the sort of person my culture promises will bring the greatest rewards. It's not only a matter of having everything our greedy hearts want, but of defining and shaping ourselves into the person we want to become—the one who will win the most prizes. The devil assures us we can do this all by our clever little selves. *Self*-indulgence, *self*-expression, *self*-fulfillment and *self*-actualization lie at the heart of our cultural agenda as we travel the path toward superhuman status through *self*-empowerment. Recently I was struck by a typical advertisement to this end.

It concerned Ralph Lauren's new perfume for young women —specifically for carefree, confident teens and twentysomethings he calls "Ralph Girls." The advertising copy for the fragrance reads, "Ralph Lauren was inspired to create RALPH by his daughter Dylan and her friends. Girls today believe in themselves, they have hopes, dreams, promise, possibilities... *and the power to make it happen*" (italics mine).[1]

Does the "Ralph Girl" and her sisters in our generation really believe she has the power to make her dreams happen? According to Ecclesiastes, "time and chance happen to them all" (9:11). Chance events can be both pleasant and unpleasant—and they certainly can determine whether or not we achieve our "dreams"! When I first came across this advertisement, I thought about how it reflected the beliefs of our culture. A common adage spouted by secular "motivational speakers" goes something like this: "You are never given a dream without also being given the power to make it come true." Really? Hearing it actually makes me incredulous. But this is what our society chooses to believe.

Is life all about being a "Ralph Girl"? Does perfume really aid you in getting what you want? You may go to your coffin smelling beautiful and with the smoothest skin and even be buried in the trendiest of clothes, but what then? According to the Teacher, "the dust returns to the ground it came from, and the spirit returns to God who gave it" (12:7). I'm all for smelling nice and looking nice. But I'm more for "being nice and doing nice." Whether it's perfume or pleasure, the delusion permeates our world: *this* is what life is all about!

No.

The *whole thing*, as we have already learned, the whole plan for fulfillment and meaning, is to "fear God and keep his commandments." Fulfillment is found in knowing a God who in the knowing gives meaning and joy to the simple things of life.

But Solomon chose, for a long period of his life, to ignore these truths. For him, to see it was to want it; to want it was to *have* to have it. Solomon had the means to do it. He did it, he had it and he came up running on empty. He was hoping to experience whatever happiness people find during their brief stay in this world. He writes, "I said to myself, 'Let's go for it—experiment with pleasure, have a good time!' But there was nothing to it, nothing but smoke" (2:1, MSG).

PROMISING MORE THAN THEY CAN DELIVER!

If the devil sees us weakening, he starts a whispering campaign right in our inner ear. "You owe it to yourself," he hisses. So we struggle on, hoping that our next achievement, our next purchase, vacation, promotion, marriage or intimate relationship will take us to an earthly Nirvana. Surely, we tell ourselves, we'll be happy once we get this that or the other; go here, there and everywhere; marry him or her; or win the jackpot! But Ecclesiastes 5:10 tells us, "whoever loves money never has money enough; whoever loves wealth is never satisfied with his income." We live in a must-have society that promises what it can't deliver while drowning out the still small voice of God. Meanwhile, the devil shouts, "You owe it to yourself to get it for yourself, to satisfy yourself!"

"Promising what it can't deliver" reminds me of being in Asia and being given a can of mosquito spray. "What does it say?" I asked, struggling to make sense of a foreign language. I was told the writing on the can was in Thai and said, "Mosquito Spray, guaranteed to make you invisible to mosquitoes." I want to tell you from bitter (bitten) experience—it was not true. The makers of the spray were promoting a lie. They promised what they could not deliver!

Solomon believed the lie, and ended up being bitten by the mosquitoes! He was sidelined by sex, possessions and ambition. He tried it all. He was an alcoholic, and a workaholic, and a success-aholic. In Ecclesiastes 2 he recounts how he decided to cheer himself with wine, and how he "undertook great projects" such as building houses, planting vineyards, designing gardens and parks, and planting fruit trees. He boasts of how he amassed wealth, acquired businesses, and had many people (slaves) working for him.

Have you undertaken great projects? Do you have many people working for you? Are you a successful business person? Are you a builder perhaps, or a landscape artist as Solomon was? Are you a success in the eyes of the world?

And if so . . . is there something missing? Has someone been robbing you blind?

The Devil Is a Robber and a Murderer

The devil wants to rob you of God—and rob God of you! He is a murderer: he kills our joy and robs our lives of significance and true satisfaction. All this time he is lying through his teeth as he tells us that all this garbage is the way to go.

"What does a man get for all the toil and anxious striving with which he labors under the sun? All his days his work is pain and grief; even at night his mind does not rest. This too is meaningless" (2:22-23). The devil kills your sleep—and that pretty well takes care of your joy! He is the quintessential insomniac and wants some company. Solomon essentially tells us that when a rich man lies down and tries to get to sleep, his body reclines but his mind sits up! Well now, Solomon would know, wouldn't he? Have you ever experienced something like that?

And just what is the rich man worrying about in the wee hours of the morning? He's wondering how to keep what he has toiled for! What a shock to realize he can't take it with him. You can't, you know.

I remember staying with Stuart's family one time. His father was sitting by the fire reading the local newspaper. The UK newspapers would print people's wills. This was always a popular piece of news!

"Did you know Mrs. Smith died?" inquired Pop of my mother-in-law as she made dinner in the kitchen.

"How much did she leave?" Mom asked.

"Everything," Pop answered, quick as a wink! Of course, we all leave everything behind. You can't take it with you. Many a man has toiled all his life and worried his nights away realizing he must leave it all, possibly to people who will squander it away. That's enough to give anyone sleepless nights! "God gives a man wealth, possessions and honor, so that he lacks nothing his heart desires, but God does not enable him to enjoy them, and a stranger enjoys them instead" (6:2).

That's frustrating! *What am I working my tail off for, when that idiot is going to blow it?* the rich man asks himself. So the devil, who is the master thief, spends his sleepless nights thinking how he can rob us of peace of mind, joy in the simple things of life that money can't buy, and of course rob us of salvation by preventing us from thinking of anything beyond the temporal. Our enemy hopes sensual and passing pleasure will be mistaken for real and lasting joy.

If perchance the devil loses a battle and someone becomes a Christian, he doesn't give up and leave that new believer alone for the rest of his life. He redoubles his efforts in order to keep the convert "worldly minded"—living, as Paul puts it, after the flesh and not after the Spirit (see Romans 8:1-13). John, writing his letter to new believers, tells them, "If anyone loves the world, the love of the Father is not in him" (1 John 2:15).

It's not only the secular person without Christ that falls into this trap. The believer is all too often robbed of joy by the devil too. Satan wants to kill any concept that living in a right relationship with God could possibly bring us joy.

I'll Never Smile Again

When I first heard of Jesus Christ and "conversion" I was doubtful about any joy involved in the whole process. In fact I thought to myself, "If I asked Christ into my life, I bet I will never smile again! Surely being *that* religious would condemn me to be miserable forever." I remember asking the girl who led me to Christ, "What will I have to give up if I become a Christian?"

"Only your sin," she replied. "Surely you can do without all that makes you miserable?"

Well, what do you do with an answer like that? I was thinking that Christ would rob me of joy, whereas it was sin that would do that.

A small boy was learning his catechism. He recited, "The whole duty of man is to know God and *endure* Him forever." To look at some believers' faces, you would think that was what it was all about! Before I became a Christian, I thought the same thing. What a wonderful surprise to learn that we get to *enjoy* God forever!

Just as we wouldn't dream of letting a burglar into our house and saying "help yourself," so we should resist the devil coming into this "heart house," helping himself to our joy and satisfaction. Don't let him do it! "Resist the devil, and he will flee from you" (James 4:7). Satisfaction comes from living rightly before God and pleasing Him, rejecting the devil's ploys.

Us Making God Happy, Not God Making Us Happy!

This is the most common mistake that is made. We think our happiness lies in God making us happy. Rather it is our task to make Him happy! When we do this we sense His pleasure. Eric Liddell, the Olympic sprinter, was quoted as saying, "God made me fast and when I run I feel His pleasure."[2] Joy is feeling God's pleasure. Joy is finding out how God made you, and training for life's Olympics with Jesus as your coach. Joy is not getting God to please me, but getting me to please God!

Living to love Him,
Dying to please Him
Sure to obey Him,
Loving to serve Him
Wanting to share Him
Longing to meet Him —
My soul singing in the rain
Dancing to the beat of His heart.
That's it! That's what life is all about!

The Devil Is a Fear Monger

As if being a liar, a thief and a murderer isn't enough, the devil is also a fear monger. There is nothing that disturbs a satisfied heart as quickly and thoroughly as fear. Some of us, believers though we be, don't experience a settled and happy spirit because we are waiting for the other shoe to drop. Reality (and the devil) says, if I am up to my chops in Erma Bombeck's cherries, it can't last—something will happen. Someone will come along and steal my last cherry and spoil everything! Fear manifests itself in worry and a low grade anxiety that doesn't quit. The result is often depression. But once someone has responded to the drawing of the Holy Spirit and moves into a vibrant and authentic relationship with God, the cycle of unbelief is broken and a new heritage of joy begins again.

The Teacher tells us there is a time for war and a time for peace (3:8). He also told us that when the time for conflict comes, there can still be peace in our hearts! The devil would give us a spirit of fear every day of our lives, but the word of God says: "For God did not give us a spirit of timidity, but a spirit of power, of love and of self-discipline" (2 Timothy 1:7). So don't accept gifts from the devil, accept gifts from God. How does this work?

Your Part and His Part

Your part in winning the battle over fear, the Teacher says, is to "banish anxiety from your heart" (11:10). Of course you can't do this in your own strength—and God does not expect you to! "The race is not to the swift or the battle to the strong" (9:11), meaning our own willpower or self-discipline is not sufficient here. We need God's power for this.

The word "banish" means "to expel from . . . a country or place by authoritative decree; condemn to exile."[3] So if you have been living with fear, God tells you to "exile" it. To tell it to get out of your life. You order it to go by the authority of the government—in this case, God. This is your part.

The dictionary uses another definition of the word *banish*. "To drive away, to forcibly dismiss—as to banish sorrow—to put out of one's thoughts as security banishes fear." Notice it says *security* banishes fear. When you are secure in the love of God, there's no room for fear and worry. Love dispels fear. To dispel means to drive away—to forcibly dismiss. So we win the battle over fear in the strength of God—the strength is God's part.

You mind your mind—and God will mind your heart.

You look after your mind by choosing to think positively. You "banish" negative thoughts, like expelling unwanted people from a country. That's our work—mind work. Paul exhorts us in Philippians 4:8, "Finally, brothers, whatever is true, whatever is noble, whatever is right, whatever is pure, whatever is lovely, whatever is admirable—if anything is excellent or praiseworthy—think about such things."

We need help to do this.

Believers have the help of the Comforter, the Holy Spirit, to banish sorrow, fear, and anxiety from the rhythm of life. When we are busy banishing worry by focusing on God and His promises, and refusing to allow fear a place to stay in "heart country," God is busy supplying our hearts with satisfaction, tranquility, and joy. When God gives a man wealth and possessions and enables him to enjoy them, to accept his lot (however hard it is) and be happy in his work (however dull it is)—this is an amazing blessing. "He seldom reflects on the days of his life, because God keeps him occupied with gladness of heart" (5:20). This is a gift of God!

How Much Is Enough?

One of the things we worry about more than any other is our money—especially if we are the bread winner. It may be we aren't greedy and want to be a spendthrift, but we struggle to make ends meet. Or, it could be that however much money we have, it's never quite enough. Listen to the Teacher. "Whoever loves money never has money enough; whoever loves wealth is never satisfied with his income" (5:10).

So we worry we will never earn enough money to fulfill our dreams or our children's dreams. Then we begin to fear what will happen if we die and the kids don't get the money we have worked so hard to bless them with. Perhaps our spouse will remarry and then everything we worked so hard for will go to a stranger's family instead of our own. The Teacher comments on this fear. "God gives a man wealth, possessions and honor, so that he lacks nothing his heart desires, but God does not enable him to enjoy them, and a stranger enjoys them instead. This is meaningless, a grievous evil" (6:2). If a man or woman can work hard, receive a wage, and do his best in life providing the best he can and trusting God for the future, then he can find peace of mind and not be driven by anxiety.

So are you satisfied with life? Do you buy into a sex-saturated, pleasure-crazy society that tells you *this* is where happiness is to be found? Did you try it all and come up empty? You are not alone! When you are ready to come to the only One who can give you a cup of cold water for your parched life, God is waiting for you in the shadows of your fruitless search.

Joy Through the Generations

As generations come and go, one here and there finds God through Christ, then marries someone who knows Him and brings up their family to know Him. Often the fervor of the first converts wanes with the generations and there can be long periods of time when Christless generations come and go. Then the prayers of the ancestors begin to be answered for their children and their children's children and the cycle begins again. Even in this greed-oriented, pleasure-seeking world, our faith and our prayers can make it possible for all generations to become believers and experience true joy.

The Teacher says, "One generation goes its way, the next one arrives, but nothing changes" (1:4, MSG). However, things *can* change. We can break the cycle of unbelief by responding to the Holy Spirit and beginning to fear God. We can change things for the future generations through our prayers. We can fortify the generations so they, like us, can stand against the materialistic and greed-obsessed society.

Years after my uncle's death I obtained his Bible. In the front he had written, "There is someone in every generation whose calling is to pray for the generations to come." My uncle prayed for me and I came to faith. His prayers were a gift!

So as you consider this whole idea of rejecting the sex-saturated, must-have culture in favor of a relationship with the Living God, don't only do it for yourself. Do it for all the generations to come!

FOR GROUP OR PERSONAL STUDY

Quietly MIND MANAGE these concepts:

1. Read Ecclesiastes 2:1-11. Meditate on it, then write a one paragraph summary in your own words. Comment in a sentence or two. What parallels do you see with our society today?
2. Read Ecclesiastes 5:10-26. What do these verses say about the one who loves money? What sort of people do riches attract? Does this remind you of one of Jesus' parables? Which one?
3. Write Ecclesiastes 5:12 in your own words. What does it mean? Can you relate this verse to your own life?
4. Read, meditate, and pray over 2 Corinthians 6:10 and 8:9.

Discussion or Journal

1. How can Ecclesiastes 5:13-16 help us to keep wealth in perspective?
2. What three things are a gift from God, according to 5:18-20? Write out 5:20 in your own words. What does this verse mean?
3. Three goals: Accept your lot in life, be happy in your work, and be content with your wages. Discuss how easy or difficult this is in your own life.
4. Compare Ecclesiastes 2:24 and 2:25. What does God give to the one who pleases Him?

Pray for Yourself and Others

- Pray for rich little poor people.
- Pray for poor little rich people!
- Pray for God's strength to seek HIM instead of wealth.

Carry Out

Think of examples of the obsession with "wine, women, and wealth" in our society. You've learned what the Teacher has to say about this. This week, keep your eyes open and try to speak God-sense into what you see around you.

SINCE ADAM WAS A LAD

Whoever loves money never has money enough; who–
ever loves wealth is never satisfied with his income.
This too is meaningless.

ECCLESIASTES 5:10

Since Adam was a lad and ate the apple,
Since Satan tempted Eve to disobey
He's promised more than he can ever give us
And tempts us all to waste our lives away.
Expecting self indulgence will bring pleasure,
We let ourselves fall hard for Satan's ploys:
We spend our hard cash on earthly treasure,
And let ourselves be fooled by Time's bright toys.

Then God came down in Christ because He loves us
And offered us forgiveness as He could:
Amazing grace showed how we find fulfillment
By dying to ourselves for others' good.
In giving we are gaining life's true riches,
In dying we are living for the Lord:
In self-forgetting service we discover
The way to self-fulfillment is assured!

Jill Briscoe
April 2006

CHAPTER 5

SEARCHING FOR SALVATION

In a Lost World

He [God] has also set eternity in the hearts of men.
ECCLESIASTES 3:11

A tribe of savage headhunters and cannibals were surprised—though pleased—to have some American visitors. These tribal people, the Sawi in New Guinea, had never seen a white man before. A young couple and their baby had taken the journey into the heart of this Stone Age people, taking incredible risks to reach them with the good news of the gospel. As the missionaries settled in and began to learn the tribal language they wondered how such a depraved race could ever understand the character of God. They began to learn the culture and when they were able to communicate, they told them the story of Jesus: His life, betrayal, death and resurrection. The tribe was fascinated with the story but much to the missionaries' chagrin, they adopted Judas, not Jesus, as their hero. Betrayal and treachery were characteristics they valued! But God had "put eternity in their hearts" and the Spirit worked. Later in an incredible turn of events, more than half the tribe converted to Christ.

There Is a Spirit Realm

The man who tells this story today—Don Richardson—was the baby those missionaries took with them to that lost tribe of people. As an adult he spent fifteen more years among the Sawi people, designing an alphabet for them, teaching them to read in their native language and translating the entire New Testament into Sawi. He wrote a book called *Peace Child* and I have seldom read such a convincing argument for the fact that God has indeed put eternity in the hearts of men and women. (In fact, Richardson wrote another book, titled *Eternity in Their Hearts.*) However depraved or sophisticated we may be, when given an opportunity to hear the good news of salvation—we respond. There is a time to be born and a time to die, and between those two events there is time to accept Christ as our Savior—if only someone will take the risk to come and tell us about Him.

There is something those savage and primitive peoples have that gives them an advantage over some of us savage "sophisticated" peoples. They can be further along in their understanding of the "other world" and far more conscious of spiritual entities than we folk in the so-called *enlightened* and developed nations. Many of them are deeply aware that there is a spirit realm that truly exists. We, on the other hand, have come "a long way baby" (or so we think) and consider ourselves too intelligent and educated to learn anything new, or to believe in all that "supernatural" stuff. Man has developed a misguided belief that we are "god enough" to care for our own soul.

MAN ISN'T GOD

The Bible states that man in all ages and on all the pages of eternal history is severely limited. He isn't God—though he is sometimes convinced he is. A man may be bright and capable, but on his own he cannot create. He isn't sovereign. He is not the Alpha and Omega, the beginning and the end. He did not make the universe, neither does he sustain it. He cannot hold everything together. He doesn't know everything nor control everything (or much of *anything*!). He cannot be in two places at the same time. He did not make himself, neither is he the source of life. He may think he can create because he can procreate, yet he can only activate the mysterious process in which God brings into being a new life. As Solomon reminds us, "As you do not know the path of the wind, or how the body is formed in a mother's womb, so you cannot understand the work of God, the Maker of all things" (Ecclesiastes 11:5).

Man doesn't have the spiritual smarts—or God-sense—to really figure out life, with or without God's Spirit! Secular man is naturally secular. He needs help from a different dimension altogether to understand the mysteries of life and death. He needs to be saved from his secular thinking, and from his natural and material mindset. Salvation means "saving." In God's grace He has put eternity in our hearts to persuade us of this truth. A longing to be saved from this earthbound "everything" appears from nowhere in our mysterious "soul realm." Nothing satisfies this eternal hunger but eternal things. It is God Himself who has placed this certainty in our hearts.

So the Holy Spirit's work draws humankind to this spiritual conclusion: "I am hungry for things I haven't found. Whatever I'm looking for, it's not found in the world in which I live and the relationships in which I am engaged. I am lonely and empty after having looked everywhere and done everything—not in the same class as Solomon, of course—but along his lines! Somehow I know 'eternity is in my heart' but I don't know what it is or what it's there for!"

It's so obvious that everyone is "searching" for the answers. Our bookstores contain shelves and shelves of self-help books. People like Dr. Phil and Dr. Laura, who seem to have all the answers, are as popular as ever. Religions like New Age, Wicca, and Scientology have exploded in recognition and membership. Meanwhile, it has become fashionable for people to engage the services of psychics, gurus and "life coaches" to help them figure out their lives. People are searching, searching, searching. We are all looking for answers.

LIFE IS FOR LOOKING FOR WHAT YOU'RE LOOKING FOR

Of course we can only search while we live. But that's what time on earth is for. Searching! Life is for looking for what you're looking for. But no matter how far and wide you search, you will come up against the truth that no person can ever love you enough, no child can ever need you enough, no job can ever satisfy you enough and no success can ever fulfill you. Only Jesus!

C. S. Lewis's famous quote began to unlock the secret of this spiritual fullness of life for me: "If I find in myself a desire which no experience in this world can satisfy, the most probable explanation is that I was made for another world."[1] This truth became real for me at conversion. A great "Ah so!" filled my heart as I lay in a hospital bed and was led to Christ by a nurse. "Ah, so this is it!" something shouted somewhere incredibly near at hand. Surprised by all these secrets, my soul began to grasp eternal dimensions and celebrate. Heaven came down and glory filled my soul! It really did, or to be more accurate, the Eternal One, Jesus Christ in the person of the Holy Spirit, came down and filled my soul. Suddenly it all made perfect sense to me! God had given me a deep-down sense of time and eternity.

LOOKING IN RELIGION

People search within their own religious philosophies. In Thailand and other Buddhist societies, we watch the search go on. Buddhism is an atheistic religion. The Buddhist says, "No god could have made such a disaster as life on this earth." The best thing is to work toward oblivion and escape the endless reincarnations that are the karma of mankind, earning sweet nothingness. The Buddhist is not supposed to believe in spirit realms in eternity.

Why then, I wondered, as we visited Buddhist temples and saw spirit houses all over the place—why try to appease capricious spirits and put streamers around trees by waterfalls to plead with the river god to be kind to us, if there is no spirit world? I'll tell you why! Somebody put eternity in their hearts.

In Bulgaria, a country staggering into freedom after fifty years of communism, I met a woman who told me that her parents had been communist officials but her grandmother was a believer. When she was a little girl her grandmother would pull her up on her knees to read to her. She would wait till no one was watching and then whisper in her ear, "God loves you!" Then she would put her finger to her lips and say, "Shh." The little girl grew up secretly cradling thoughts about God's love deep in her heart.

As a young woman with her grandmother gone, she was witness to the revolution, the fall of communism and newfound liberty. One day as she was shopping, western Christians came to her town to preach the gospel and hand out Bibles in the market squares, and she came upon a street preacher talking about the love of God from John 3:16. She stood riveted to the spot. Afterward she walked up to the man and asked, "Sir, can you tell me about the God who loves me?" She came to Christ and soon was interpreting for our meetings! Somebody had put "eternity in her heart" and her heart had waited patiently to hear how she could realize that truth.

Stuart and I were visiting Australia. We had been there many times, and this time we were fascinated with the story of Arthur Stace, a down and out Australian who had become a legend. We had played tourist for half a day, visiting Parliament House and the museum in Canberra. Inside there was a permanent exhibition about the multicultural spirituality of Australia. It displayed human-interest stories under the headings of hope, persistence, love, courage, and so on, telling tales of their heritage and culture. All were under one huge word, "Eternity," written in beautiful copperplate script (an elegant script similar to calligraphy). Here in this tourist Mecca is a grand God-honoring story of evangelical faith. This one stunning word, "Eternity," was strung across the Sydney Harbour Bridge the night the world watched the birth of the New Millennium on television. You may well have seen it too!

The museum tells the story in words and pictures of Arthur Stace who, back in 1930, was a homeless alcoholic on his last legs when he staggered into a church—probably for the free food—and walked out converted to Christianity. Two years later Stace heard a stirring message about eternity by Rev. John Ridley. "Eternity, Eternity, I wish that I could sound or shout that word to everyone in the streets of Sydney," the preacher cried. Arthur Stace complied.

As Stace said, "Eternity went ringing through my brain and suddenly I began crying and felt a powerful call from the Lord to write Eternity." He walked out of the church and, finding a piece of chalk in his pocket, bent down and wrote "Eternity" on the sidewalk. While Stace was illiterate at the time, "It came out smoothly, in a beautiful copperplate script. I couldn't understand it, and I still can't," he later recalled. For the next thirty-seven years, he wrote the word all over the streets of Sydney, on sidewalks, train stations and anywhere else he felt led to—over half a million times in all. It has become part of the city's culture and the story of his radical life change through faith in Jesus Christ is told in the Canberra museum. The story is—more importantly—written on the hearts of men and women who have visited Sydney, Australia, over the years and been alerted to the fact that *God has put eternity in the hearts of men and women!* [2]

What Am I Doing with My Piece of Chalk?

So what am I doing with my piece of chalk on the pavements of my world? I asked myself as I stood in front of the pictures and words about Arthur Stace and watched the public drop by to read, ponder, and move on. (You can even buy a mug with the word on it in the gift shop!)

I left for the USA shortly afterward, having the most interesting and productive conversation with a lovely young girl on the flight home. She told me she was a "spiritual counselor" in the corporate world, credentialed by a university in Sydney. The crystals round her neck told me we weren't on the same page though we had a lively conversation! (She had been reseated next to me after the flight took off, which led me to welcome her with interest and a prayer.) She and I talked and debated most of the way home, and left each other with unfinished business that I pray the Lord allows me to complete in the future.

She helped me to see all over again that God is at work in the hearts of men and women—whatever their belief system or lack thereof. You cannot jettison this secret knowledge at will, pretend it isn't there, or ignore its sweet insistence to search for life's answers. You cannot resist the irrefutable eternal truth that just won't stop insisting, "You are made for another world!"

God has set this sense of eternal importance in our hearts so we will give up the quest for profit (or "surplus gain") for its own sake and truly seek God. Somebody put Eternity in my heart! Somebody put Eternity in *your* heart! So as the world is turning in the normal everyday doings and goings, the rhythm of life beats out an insistent message—but in this "here and now" we are insufficient for the task of truly understanding it. It is a message of eternity, and only God can reveal it. Yet—we live as if the here and now is eternal, and the eternal is temporary, as if we had all the time in the world to play with our toys!

WHAT ON EARTH IS ETERNITY DOING IN MY HEART?

The devil uses the most normal things to try and distract us from these life-changing discoveries. Chapter 3 of Ecclesiastes describes the usual rhythm of life: the living and the dying, the planting and the harvesting, the healing and the dying, the fighting and the truce making, the weeping and laughing, mourning and dancing. The devil tries to use the rituals and cycles of life to take our minds off of Eternity.

Yet most of the people I know have found their destiny in the middle of the muddle of life with all its distractions, *while* they are loving and hating, making war or peace, even while falling in love or out of it. The things with which the devil tries to distract us are never enough to stop the human spirit asking, "Where is it? What is it? Why is it? What on earth is eternity doing in my heart?" It must drive the devil to despair!

The devil is a master of illusion, confusion and delusion. If he fails to keep your mind on a short leash and it gets to ponder the imponderable, and you begin to search with all your heart, soul, mind and strength for answers to life, he panics! He has failed to make you believe you can be the master of your own destiny, determining how long you'll live, the manner of your demise, and what you'll do with the goods that accrue through your hard work, hoarding or luck! He has miserably failed to make you believe "this is all there is"! It's not so—and you know it! The fool has stopped being a fool and has become wise. Satan has lost his victim.

One day Jesus spoke to this point using a parable. He had been teaching, and afterward a man came to Him and said, "Teacher, tell my brother to divide the inheritance with me." Jesus warned the man, "Watch out! Be on your guard against all kinds of greed; a man's life does not consist in the abundance of his possessions" (Luke 12:13-15).

He told a story about a farmer who became rich and indulgent and one day said to himself, "You have plenty of good things laid up for many years. Take life easy; eat, drink and be merry" (Luke 12:19). Jesus said the man was a fool because that very night his life would be demanded from him and all his hoarding would have done him no good—it would have been a waste of time. Worse, the man's riches would probably be inherited by people who didn't deserve them! Jesus was speaking a warning to "anyone who stores up things for himself but is *not rich toward God*" (Luke 12:21, italics mine).

Ecclesiastes 8:8 tells us, "No one has power over the day of his death." In other words, you can't keep yourself alive! I was unaware of these Scriptures as I lay seriously ill in a hospital bed. I was all of eighteen years of age and it began to dawn on me that no one could figure out what was wrong with me. There was something wrong—that much was obvious! I had a temperature that wouldn't come down to normal, a biting pain in my stomach and I felt terrible. Thinking it was my appendix, they rid me of the offending organ only to find out the pain didn't quit and the temperature didn't drop. So they concluded it wasn't that and consulted with more puzzled doctors.

I began to feel more and more out of control. After all, I was only eighteen. This was getting beyond a joke. It was not funny! My mind circled around a horrible thought that I didn't know, my parents didn't know and the hospital didn't know how to keep me alive. I began to panic. Eventually someone figured out I had a kidney problem, but in a day and age when kidneys were not available, transplants having not been imagined, and dialysis was not on the radar screen, this was not welcome news.

God used this outward circumstance to turn me "inward" to confront a soul that had been like the farmer making his own merry little plans to be thoroughly self-centered, self-indulgent and self-satisfied. I had played the fool and I knew it. Having been forced in my extremity to look inward, I was then drawn to look upward to a God I somehow knew had been waiting in the shadows of my life to call me into a relationship that would stand me on my head—a relationship with Him. The options, although I did not know the biblical words to describe them, were, "This very night your life will be demanded from you" (Luke 12:20) or "Now is the day of salvation" (2 Corinthians 6:2). There was no contest! Years ago I heard a story that made the same point.

THE RICHEST MAN IN THE VALLEY

There was a man who was the richest farmer in the valley. He was not a God-fearing man but was instead a "self-made" man who worshipped his creator (himself!). He had in his employ a humble gardener who loved the Lord.

One day the richest man in the valley opened the door to his godly servant who stood outside on the doorstep holding his hat awkwardly in his hands.

"What is it?" his master asked him.

"Sir," the man replied awkwardly, "I had a dream that tonight at midnight the richest man in the valley would die."

"Why, my man," the richest man in the valley replied, "I'm in excellent health—don't you worry about me!" Then gently, "It's all that religion you go in for—makes you think morbid thoughts."

The man shuffled away and the master went inside the house again. However, he couldn't get over the man's words and he decided to stay up late and ask his friend the doctor to come over and play bridge with him—just in case! The doctor complied and the evening passed with the richest man in the valley glancing at the clock every half hour or so and insisting the doctor stay and play just "one more game."

At half past midnight the doctor left and the richest man in the valley chided himself for being so foolish. As he turned off the lights and started to go up the winding staircase to bed, the doorbell rang. Thinking the doctor had forgotten something, the rich man returned to the front door and opened it. A young girl stood weeping on the doorstep.

"Whatever is the matter?" the man inquired, not unkindly.

"Sir," the girl replied, "tonight at midnight my father died."

"Who is your father?" the richest man in the valley asked.

"Your gardener, sir," she said.

The richest man in the valley! And indeed he was, for those who know and love the Lord are rich beyond measure—in this world and the next.

We can be as poor as a church mouse as far as this world's goods are concerned, but wealthy in "God things." There are spiritual riches, the Bible says, that surpass anything the world can offer. Jesus asks in Mark 8:36, "What good is it for a man to gain the whole world, yet forfeit his soul?"

I Am the Poker Champion of America!

I meet the most fascinating people when I travel. Once on a flight in America I sat beside a man who was extremely "colorful"—he told me he was the poker champion of America. Looking at him, I believed him!

"That's fascinating," I said. "Tell me about it." He proceeded to do so for a couple of hours! During the course of this, he mentioned "the Man upstairs" who had seen him right and given him luck. He owned a chunk of Las Vegas, houses, toys, and pleasures. He had a beautiful wife who loved him, and kids who were following along happily in his footsteps. In his own mind, he had certainly included the "God" factor into his "poker driven" life.

I was able to engage him in debate and asked him what he would think of God if his luck ran out on earth, and if he got to heaven and discovered he wasn't going to be let through the pearly gates. He assured me that if God had seen him right up to this point, he couldn't see why God wouldn't continue to make sure his luck lasted till he got to "his appointed mansion in the sky" (in which mansion I am sure he expected to be equipped with a gaming table—his idea of heaven!).

"On what basis do you expect to get there?" I asked him.

"God knows I'm a generous guy," he replied. "He knows I've given more than my share of nickels to the United Way."

"Well," I said, "that's not going to get you there." And I told him about the narrow gate and was able to explain the gospel.

"I'll take my chances," he replied when I'd finished.

"I can't believe a veteran gambler like you would take that sort of a risk," I replied. I had his attention. *"Don't gamble with your soul,"* I said gently. "The stakes are too high."

THE MAN UPSTAIRS

There are more than a few "upstairs-downstairs" people who have a concept of God that is far short of the revealed Father God of Scripture. My poker-loving friend was one of them. As I talked with him, however, I hoped he saw that to have a concept so far short of the Holy God who would bring everything into judgment at the end of the "game" was a gamble not worth taking. In this man I heard the heart cry of Solomon.

Walter C. Kaiser, in his book *Total Life*, said,

> This quest is a deep-seated desire, a compulsive drive. Man has an inborn inquisitiveness and capacity to learn how every-thing in his experience can be integrated to make a whole. He wants to know how the mundane 'downstairs' realm of the ordinary day to day living fits with the 'upstairs' realm of the hereafter—how the business of living, eating, working, and enjoying, can be made to fit with the call to worship, serve and love the living God.[3]

In the middle of life as we live it, no matter what creed we adhere to or what culture we are of, there is this inner reach for something unreachable; a search for the unsearchable; a desire to comprehend the incomprehensible, and unscrew the inscrutable! Above all there is this secret knowledge there is someone, somewhere, *waiting* for us; and a feeling that we should have come sooner to meet Him. This is universal!

Next time you go to the grocery store, watch the young mother with her kid in the checkout line in front of you. Look at her with new eyes. Someone put eternity in her heart. When you grab a coffee at your local coffeehouse, see the eyes of the young barista. Are they bored and impassive with no spark or purpose? Somebody put eternity in his heart. Take a moment to smile at him and see if he might respond to a word of positive encouragement. Remember—inside this boy there is the awareness of something missing—the God-shaped hole that looks for substance. Carry a New Testament to give away, a small booklet, or an invitation to church. You may be surprised how many people would respond to such a thing.

This whole concept of eternity being in the heart of men has changed most of my journeys—even to the grocery store—into adventures. As you go about the daily "round and round," go with expectation that someone doesn't know where the answers to their searching hearts are to be found. Pray that God will bring people across your path whom He knows are waiting and willing to receive something from you. It surely transforms your day!

Maybe you are a school teacher. Look over your classroom at all those little eternal people sitting in front of you and see them with new eyes. "But," you say, "we aren't allowed to proselytize in the class-room!" I know. I was a teacher in the British school system. Every day I had a chance to say something to someone about Him. If there was interest I would ask them to drop by my classroom after school so I could give them something to read.

As a teacher out in the playground (we teachers used to call it vice patrol!) or after school hours, the relationships made in the classroom could be used to encourage a child who was hurting; find help for the one being bullied; reach out to the ones heading in the wrong direc-tion; and generally explain (as the opportunity arose) why there was a longing for something more, something better, something their souls were reaching for. Someone (and I knew Who) had put eternity in their hearts!

I was led to Christ by a nurse. When she was working she found ways to talk to many patients a day about the Lord. Using tact and choosing your moments, you can share the truth of God in the marketplace, the workplace, the classroom or wherever you go.

God has implanted eternal awareness of Himself. We have it when we are playing, working, or when we are living or dying. When we are weeping or when we are laughing; when we are mourning or when we are dancing; when we are searching or when we give up. It's an inside-outside thing, an upstairs-downstairs thing.

MY SPRINGS OF OPTIMISM ARE DRY

A man I had been working with had come to the Lord but was disillusioned with the church and Christians and life in general. One day he told me, "My springs of optimism are dry. There is nothing left. I'm leaving the church."

You can leave the church and the fellowship of believers and try and isolate yourself from Christian culture, but you can't tear out of your heart the eternal "knowings" planted firmly in your soul by a God who loves you too much to let you go! Leaving the church won't solve your problems.

But what if you really feel like your "springs of optimism are dry"? Time to go back to the part about doing some "mind work" and deciding to change your attitude. Time to practice thinking about things that are good about the church, good about people, good in the world around you. You'll want to invite the Spirit to change your heart and give you grace to get you through this valley. The problem with the church is that it is full of people! Sometimes we wallow in being dry and somehow receive gratification from our resentment, disillusionment and pessimism. We just have a pity party—after all, it's easier than actually dealing with our heart-attitudes that allowed us to get here! We don't want to deal with our judgment, unforgiveness, and so on.

The truth is, we need to deal honestly with all these aspects of ourselves. Why? Because God has put Eternity in our hearts, and that nagging craving for more is not going to go away. As we've seen throughout this chapter, only a vibrant relationship with the Living God will satisfy. He is the answer to all our longings!

FOR GROUP OR PERSONAL STUDY

Quietly MIND MANAGE these concepts:
1. Which of the following subheads spoke to you most poignantly?
   - There Is a Spirit Realm
   - Man Isn't God
   - Life Is for Looking for What You're Looking for
   - My Springs of Optimism Are Dry

   Consider what each one said to you.
2. Read Ecclesiastes 3:1-11. What does this passage mean to you? Pick your favorite verse and put it into your own words. Ponder.
3. What are you doing with your piece of chalk? Is there any way in which you are writing "Eternity" where other people can see it? How could you do this better?

Discussion or Journal
1. Read John 3:16. How do you obtain everlasting life?
2. Read 1 John 1:1-4. List the things you learn about Eternal life.
3. What does it mean to "believe"? How would you explain John 3:16 in your own words to someone who has never heard the gospel? Discuss or write.

Pray for Yourself and Others
- If you are in a group, stay still and quiet to allow people to pray on their own. Perhaps some will pray to accept Jesus as their Savior. Help them to do that. The poem following this section can be used as a prayer.
- Pray that God would show you exactly how He wants you to share Eternity with others. Ask Him to bring others into your presence who need to hear about Him.
- Pray that your springs of optimism do not run dry!

Carry Out

Read Revelation 3:20. Make sure you have received the Spirit of God. You can do it by simply asking Him in prayer to come into your life. This week, make a list of all the ways you can be sure He came in. Share them at the next meeting, or write about them in your journal.

THANK YOU, LORD

*He has planted eternity in the human heart, but even
so, people cannot see the whole scope of God's work
from beginning to end.*

ECCLESIASTES 3:11, NLT

Loving Jesus heavenly Savior
See this sinner needing You,
Please forgive the sinful actions
You have told me not to do.

Please come in my heart Lord Jesus
See I open up the door;
Enter Spirit take possession
Tell me what you have in store.

Thank You Lord you heard this sinner
Searching, empty, lonely lost;
Thank You Lord, You died to save me
Took my place at such a cost.

Help me now to live a lifestyle
Showing men Salvations gain,
Use me Lord to tell Your story
To a world in tears and pain.

Jill Briscoe

CHAPTER 6

SEARCHING FOR A SOUL MATE

In a Lonely World

> *Two are better than one, because they have a good return for their work: If one falls down, his friend can help him up. But pity the man who falls and has no one to help him up! Also, if two lie down together, they will keep warm. But how can one keep warm alone? Though one may be overpowered, two can defend themselves. A cord of three strands is not quickly broken.*
>
> ECCLESIASTES 4:9-12

The Teacher declares there are huge advantages of companion-ship. Society begins with one's neighbor. This wisdom applies to all our relationships and is certainly relevant for members of the body of Christ. Two acting together are better than one selfish individual; they can support each other when there is need for help and encouragement.

Individualism, selfish hidden agendas, and divisions make for weakness. There is an added strength and power in a three-strand rope, provided the strands are healthy and support one another. There is a saying from the Talmud, "A man without a companion is like a left hand without the right."[1] In other words, a person without a friend is like someone with one hand tied behind their back.

Two Are Better Than One

But what are the elements of real friendship? Friends are not always a blessing. We can get caught up with the wrong people. And which parent has not watched a negative friendship threaten to destroy their child? There is no doubt, however, that here the Teacher is showing us the positive aspects of real friendship and companionship.

The whole subject of friendship is worth thinking seriously about. Have we ever evaluated our own qualities as a friend? It could help to ask ourselves how we would rate. Would we see ourselves as forgiving, supportive, trusting, a gossip? Are we good listeners, affectionate, and thoughtful—or jealous and possessive? Maybe we are bossy, humorless and not much fun! Are we loyal and to be trusted with a secret, or not one to keep our mouths shut? Are we insecure, inflexible or angry? Can we see ourselves as others see us? And how would our friends rate us? Ask them—and be willing to hear what they have to say!

Years ago I had a wonderful friend. She was on staff at the same youth mission Stuart and I served. She and I began to reach out to the kids in the town nearby. It was exciting and the work grew. I took the lead and she followed. She assisted me and put feet to my dreams and ideas. I was the leader and she was the follower.

By nature I am bossy! It just comes naturally and that's the problem. Bossiness always comes naturally and not spiritually! So one day as we were planning an event and my friend and I were working on the details, I said to her, "Just run down to the kitchen and see if the food is ready to take down to the youth center."

I didn't say please, I just told her to get going and do it. She didn't move. I looked up a little surprised and said, "You'd better hurry, we're going soon." She still didn't jump to it and instead said quietly, "I like to be asked, not told, Jill."

"Oh dear, I'm so sorry!" I said at once, aghast at my tone and attitude. She'd quite rightly called me on it. That's what friends do. "Iron sharpens iron," so the Good Book says (Proverbs 27:17) and "Wounds from a friend can be trusted" (Proverbs 27:6). What sort of a friend are you? True friendship is a safe place to say such things to each other.

SIDE BY SIDE IN MINISTRY

There is no better place to develop deep friendships than in ministry. When you work side by side in a venture for the Lord, a depth of companionship results. A dictionary definition of a friend is, "one attached to another by affection or esteem; one that is not hostile; one that is of the same nation, party, or group; a favored companion."[2]

Such is the nature of friendship. To labor for Jesus and the kingdom together not only creates a bond that is strong and lasting, but brings results for God's work that one on his or her own would not be able to accomplish. Ecclesiastes 4:9 says, "Two are better than one, because they have a good return for their work." There is a bond formed when two strive together to accomplish a common goal for God.

Those of you who find it hard to find friends, look around in the body of Christ. Investigate your relationships at church—start there. Invite someone to join you in a spiritual endeavor. Volunteer for a project together. Look in the ministries going on and throw yourself into helping. This will bring you into touch with people who have similar passions and beliefs, giving you a solid foundation from which friendship can grow. Such opportunities to assist abound. It might even be your friendships will grow from among the people you serve and not the leaders with whom you serve.

If we are usually the leader and not the follower, it is also very good for us to be in a serving capacity somewhere else. There is an old saying: *"It takes more grace than I can tell, to play the second fiddle well."*[3] This is true especially when you have "first fiddle gifts," as my friend who assisted me in the youth work had! She faithfully served me for years and when I left the ministry to emigrate to the USA, she took over the work and it continued seamlessly and grew under her leadership. She had all the first fiddle gifts, but chose to play a symphony of humility in her position in the work with me.

God has told me in no uncertain terms to find a "second fiddle place" somewhere in ministry, no matter what "first fiddle place" I am filling. This, He tells me, is for my own heart's good!

FRIENDSHIP GIVES US AN ACCOUNTABILITY PARTNER

Friendship also gives us a chance to be accountable to someone. There should be no mavericks in God's Kingdom work; no loose cannons on the deck. But unfortunately you know as well as I do that there are! We can say to our friends in ministry, "Keep my feet to the fire; keep me loyal, keep me honest; keep me reaching for a star, and I will do the same for you." A good friend holds us accountable.

So, "two are better than one" because they have a good return for their labor—a good return for their work. Two people can accomplish twice as much as one, hold each other accountable and share the work and enjoy the fruits of it.

I wrote a book about friendship a while back—now out of print—that was my "thank you" to some friends in my life. Looking back, as I think about the friends I chose to write about, most of them were in ministry with me. Look around and pray that God will give you some way to serve Jesus and find lasting friendships at the same time!

"Ministry" is another way of saying "serving Jesus," and Stuart and I have a life verse that has been a real bellwether test of how we are doing in this regard. It comes from the book of Joshua, and says, "As for me and my household, we will serve the LORD" (24:15).

Another favorite verse of ours is, "One man [will] chase a thousand, or two put ten thousand to flight" (Deuteronomy 32:30). Stuart and I reckoned that two of us could make the devil sorry he started this mess in the first place! Our friendship has flourished as we have served Jesus together for nearly fifty years. Ministry goes better when we are friends doing it together, and friendship does better when two are serving Him.

MY HUSBAND, MY FRIEND

Though Ecclesiastes 4:9 ("Two are better than one") doesn't specifically talk about the marriage relationship, it is often quoted in a wedding ceremony. And that's legitimate. Too seldom is this aspect of marriage emphasized in marriage counseling or preparation for marriage. Many marriages are "friendless" arrangements, empty of the companionship that lasts when "eros" might grow cold. Eros, the sensual side of love, waxes and wanes, but friendship can hold a marriage together until eros can be ignited again.

I remember Stuart and I talking to our children about this aspect of their relationships as they took off into the wild blue yonder of college. We talked about how building a solid foundation of friendship is so important. "Do you like being together?" Stuart asked Judy and her boyfriend. "Do you delight in each other? Have common interests?" We tried to tell them that the sexual side of marriage is very important but not all-important. Most of our married hours are spent not in bed but in "doing life together"! I know people who tell us, "We have a good sex life but hardly say a thing to each other all day!" What's more, they choose to spend their leisure hours with friends rather than with their spouse because they really don't like each other's company very much. That doesn't sound to me like the recipe for a successful marriage!

Our daughter Judy called home after four years at Wheaton College. She had dated Greg all that time. She asked her Daddy, "Can I marry my best friend?" What a wonderful question! Stuart was able to say the sexual side needed to be there too, but how delighted he was that these two young people, knowing they had a long haul ahead of them till they could get married, were first building a solid wonderful friendship together where they had learned to thoroughly enjoy each other. In marriage "two are better than one" not only because our God-given sexual needs can be satisfied, but because the need for deep companionship is satisfied too.

FACE TO FACE

Another reason two are better than one is that they can support each other when things are difficult. In ministry and in misery, friends can make the difference.

A further definition of a friend is that of a *supporter* or *sympathizer*. Friends face things together. Friends watch out for each other and are there for each other if one is struggling. "If one falls down, his friend can help him up. But pity the man who falls and has no one to help him up!" (4:10).

David and Jonathan come readily to mind. Saul, jealous of David's growing popularity with the people, was trying to kill David. While David was in hiding, Jonathan (Saul's son) went to him and "strengthened his hand in God" (1 Samuel 23:16, KJV). That's what friends do for friends! The Bible says that Jonathan loved David deeply and encouraged him at a lonely and hard place in his life.

I edit a magazine for ministry wives and women in leadership. One of the top needs of this group of women is for a "Jonathan" in their lives. They tell us they are lonely, as their husbands are constantly called upon to be a friend to everyone in the congregation, and can hardly find the time or energy to be a friend to their own wives.

One of my friends, a pastor's wife, wrote an article about feeling as though there was another woman in her husband's life. She meant the church! "He dresses for the other woman," she wrote. "He is on time for the other woman. He takes care of the other woman's children before his own!" You get the picture.

Having been a pastor's wife for thirty-seven years, I understand! There is all the more reason for the pastor and his wife to nourish their friendship, but it is also an opportunity for a wife to find a Jonathan. When hard things happen in the church family or our husband is away in ministry, we desperately need a friend to help us find strength in God, as Jonathan did for David.

Do you know anyone in ministry who needs a friend? (Like your pastor's wife, perhaps?) Why not offer her the gift of friendship? I would encourage you to take the initiative. As Qoheleth says in the *New Living Translation*, "If one person falls, the other can reach out and help. But someone who falls alone is in real trouble" (4:10).

There is a tendency for people to isolate themselves when sad, depressed, or recovering from crisis or failure. I have noticed this especially in Christians! We sometimes have the feeling, "I don't need anyone. Together, God and I can handle it." But God "sets the lonely in families" (Psalm 68:6). This means our own family and God's family, the group of believers in our community. We are there for mutual support and encouragement. When the family or the church neglects to do its part in comforting and encouraging us, we tend to isolate and cut ourselves off from help. Try not to do that, even if you have been hurt or disappointed by people from whom you expected help. Ask God to show you someone with whom to connect.

Are you in "real trouble" because you do not have a good friend? I trust God will give you a friend not only in your marriage, but outside of it too. A friend who will strengthen your hand in God.

What are some other aspects of true friendship? True friends give each other a second chance. A biblical example of this is that of Barnabas and John Mark.

One Strike and You're Out

Paul had taken along John Mark, a young "assistant," on his first missionary journey with Barnabas. Barnabas's name means "son of encouragement" and his name was as good as his nature. When John Mark withdrew from the enterprise and went home at a critical moment leaving Paul and Barnabas without help, Paul was angry. So angry that when the next opportunity came to choose the team to travel on another missionary journey, Paul would not think about giving young John Mark a second chance. In effect he said, "One strike and you're out." Barnabas, however, went to bat for the boy, and the feeling was so strong between the two veterans over the issue that they parted company. Paul took Silas as his assistant and Barnabas took John Mark.

What would have happened if Barnabas had not "strengthened the hand" of John Mark at that crucial point? Barnabas gave the young man, who'd had a failure of nerve, the freedom to fail. True friends give people a second chance. Barnabas probably saved young Mark for the Christian church—and Mark went on to write the fourth gospel! Proverbs 17:17 says, "a friend loves at all times." Not just the good times, but the hard times and the discouraging times too. Friends help friends when the cold winds blow. Paul ended up reconciled to young John Mark, who became his helper in his old age. A good ending to the story!

Bracing Against the Cold

In the Teacher's world, while traveling together on cold nights companions would sleep close together to survive the weather. There were also bandits around. Trouble on the roads was a common danger that faced the ancient traveler, and "two were better than one" to face the enemy. There was the need of companionship in adversity. "How can one keep warm alone?" the Teacher asks rhetorically (4:11). As two try to keep warm under the same blanket at night, so two can give each other not only body heat but "soul heat" as well!

Stuart and I were invited to go on a fantastic adventure trip to Antarctica. We saw Creation as we had never seen it before. We were there in summer, but we were told that in winter, upward of a million penguins huddle together in a mass in their breeding grounds, their backs turned against the bitter arctic blast, their bodies sharing life-giving warmth and shelter to each other and their young. Incredibly, year after year they survive.

When we find ourselves in the arctic adversity of life—huddled against the wind of cruel circumstance—family breakdown, disappointment or grief—we need other "penguin" friends that will lend us their "soul heat" and stand side by side against the elements.

ENEMIES OF FRIENDSHIP

We can learn from the Bible what strengthens relationships and what kills them. For example, taking offense easily kills friendship. Amy Carmichael, in her little booklet *If*, says, "If I take offense easily—if I am content to continue in a cool unfriendliness though friendship be possible, then I know nothing of Calvary love." Again Amy says, "If I do not give a friend the benefit of the doubt but put the worst construction instead of the best on what is said or done, then I know nothing of Calvary love." And, "If I can hurt another by speaking faithfully without much preparation of spirit and without hurting myself far more than I hurt that other, then I know nothing of Calvary love."[4]

Ruth Bell Graham is often quoted as saying, "A happy marriage is the union of two good forgivers."[5] Good forgivers make good friends too. This is not contradicting what I have said about saying things that need to be said. Remember, "faithful are the wounds of a friend" (Proverbs 27:6, KJV). But when necessary hard things are said, afterward forgiveness is needed to heal the rough edges of those painful conversations. Sometimes we even have to forgive our friends for being faithful friends and telling us the truth!

David had two good friends, Jonathan and Nathan. Jonathan loved David to death. In Jonathan's eyes, David could do no wrong. We all need that sort of a friend. Nathan loved David too. But when David did something wrong, Nathan called him on it! We need a "Nathan" too.

Encouragement isn't always "soft." I well remember a great friend of mine listening to my litany of woes and then saying firmly but kindly, "Have a good cry, then wash your face, get up, and get on with it." It worked. The word "encourage" means to "put courage into." She surely put it into me!

We also need to *be* a Jonathan and a Nathan for others, as well as looking for those types of friends for ourselves. In fact, if we try to offer these two elements of friendship we will probably find the friends we are looking for. In other words, be a friend and you will find a friend!

A friend loves at all times, and it is this element of "Calvary love," as Amy Carmichael puts it, that helps us listen to our friends' loving encouragement and act on it. Paul said, "I have you in my heart" (Philippians 1:7) and then proceeded to correct and rebuke his friends. When you know someone loves you and has you in their heart, you can hear their words of correction. It's called "speaking the truth in love" (Ephesians 4:15) or sometimes we call it "leveling in love" but when it happens you aren't "leveled."

Friendship needs to be based on biblical principles, and it also needs to be practical. For example, we can offer words of encouragement but we also need to think of concrete ways to help. It's more than talk—it's offering a meal if your friend is sick, a ride in your car if she needs it, help with her kids if she is exhausted and needs a break. Sometimes your help will be verbal. As Ecclesiastes warns, however, there is "a time to be silent and a time to speak" (3:7).

A friend of mine took a risk on our friendship by talking to me about a problem that had arisen. First (she told me afterward), she fasted and prayed abut whether to talk to me at all. That is a good start. Second she told me she decided she would not say anything more than she had to say. The old saying, "The less said, the sooner mended" is a very sound principle! My friend did it right, and said it right, and I was pleased to respond to her.

LIFE IS NOT A PLAYGROUND, IT IS A BATTLEGROUND

Friends are necessary in the battleground of life. Life for the believer is a battleground—not a playground! We need to stand side by side, face to face, and back to back to beat the enemy of our souls!

A friend is a person on the same side in a struggle. Allies, opposed to foes. In a battle, individualism and division make for weakness, whereas unity strengthens. "Though one may be overpowered, two can defend themselves" (4:12).

We do have an enemy who is out to destroy us. We make his job easier if there are divisions of our own making that we refuse to mend within our ranks. True friendship guards against that. If you act separately, both may be torn apart.

The ancient Britons were invaded by the Romans. While they fought in detached parties they sacrificed the general cause. Once they got together and stayed together they made progress. The same is true for us. Two can keep a lookout. "Watch your back!" they can shout. And of course, the more friends the better.

In 1 Chronicles 19, David's armies are fighting battles with both the Arameans and the Ammonites. Joab was in command of the troops fighting the Arameans and Abishai, his brother, was in command of the troops fighting the Ammonites. Joab said to his brother, "If the Arameans are too strong for me, then you are to rescue me; but if the Ammonites are too strong for you, then I will rescue you. Be strong and let us fight bravely for our people and the cities of our God. The LORD will do what is good in his sight" (verses 12-13). Basically he was saying, *you help me against my enemy, and I'll help you against yours!*

What was the result of two friends watching out for each other's backs? Both the Ammonites and the Arameans fled (see verses 14-15). In the *New Living Translation* the Teacher reminds us: *"A person standing alone can be attacked and defeated, but two can stand back-to-back and conquer"* (4:12).

PEOPLE ARE NOT THE ENEMY

Sisters and brothers in Christ are not the enemy—although the real enemy would have us think so. Satan is the enemy and we must recognize his way of messing things up. He hates friendship as God has intended it to be, because he knows the power of it.

I have a close friend who was having trouble with a difficult person in her church. They were friends and both were in leadership. She told me, "You know, we don't agree on how this particular program should be run—or how to accomplish the plan—but I realized this division is not caused by my friend, but is the scheme of the devil wanting division among us. I've decided I'm going to take her to coffee and talk it out." She followed through and was able to say to her friend, "We're both after the same thing, so let's recognize who is causing this rift!" *She stopped looking at the person as the enemy.* Remember who you are fighting! Peter was unaware Satan was using him when Jesus said, "Get behind me, Satan!" (Matthew 16:23). Jesus did not say, "Peter, you are Satan"; He said, "Satan—you are Satan, and I recognize you and what you are trying to do." Friends can help friends to recognize the enemy.

The word "friend" is associated with such words as benevolence, kindness, rapport, amicable. Not hostile, but helpful and sympathetic. Don't just *look* for a friend with these characteristics—be one! Remember, to find a friend, you must first be friendly.

DON'T BE EXCLUSIVE WITH YOUR FRIENDSHIPS

Always make room for more friends. Investigate the friendships you have already, and widen the circle. Be inclusive, not exclusive. "A cord of three strands is not quickly broken" (4:12).

Finally, give your friendships room to breathe. Don't be possessive. Amy Carmichael says, "If, in the fellowship of service I seek to attach a friend to myself, so that others are caused to feel unwanted; if my friendships do not draw others deeper in, but are ungenerous (that is to myself, for myself) then I know nothing of Calvary love."[6] Calvary love is always concerned with the other's well-being, irrespective of the cost to self. Calvary love freshens all friendships. Jesus in the end is the three-fold cord that binds a friendship together!

FOR GROUP OR PERSONAL STUDY

Quietly MIND MANAGE these concepts:

1. Read Ecclesiastes 4:9-12 again. Without looking at the lesson or your notes, list all the reasons you can remember that "two are better than one."
2. What sort of a friend are you? Do you have a lot of friends? What do you look for in a friend?
3. What does "Calvary love" mean to you? What are some ways you can make this a reality in your life and relationships?

Discussion or Journal

Look up and discuss the following verses. What do you learn about friendship from them?

1. Exodus 33:11
2. Proverbs 17:17
3. Proverbs 18:24
4. Proverbs 27:6
5. Proverbs 16:28
6. John 15:13

Pray for Yourself and Others

- Pray for your friends.
- Pray for friends for yourself and your family.
- Pray for fractured friendships—in marriage, in church.
- Pray for your children's friendships.

Carry Out

Write out one thing you will do from the lesson to make a new friendship, mend a broken friendship, or start a new friendship. Follow through! Maybe you could send this book with this poem to your friend!

TO MY FRIEND

If one falls down his friend can help him up —
But pity the man who falls and has no one to help him up!

ECCLESIASTES 3:10

Thank you for being a friend of mine
For sticking with me in the heat of the day
Thank you for being a friend of mine-
Come what may!

Thank you for being a challenging friend
For facing me up with the issues of life.
Thank you for being a challenging friend
In the strife!

Thank you for being a patient friend
For holding your peace when I'm being a fool
Thank you for being a patient friend
That's cool!

Thank you for being a godly friend,
For loving the Lord and serving Him true
Thank you for being a godly friend
Thank you for you!

Jill Briscoe

CHAPTER 7

SEARCHING FOR SOCIAL JUSTICE

In an Unjust World

> *There is something else meaningless that occurs on earth: righteous men who get what the wicked deserve, and wicked men who get what the righteous deserve.*
>
> ECCLESIASTES 8:14

If I'm searching for significance there's a good chance I'll find it by getting involved with those less fortunate than me. Strangely enough—as I give, I receive. As I die, I live. As I spend myself on behalf of others, I find money in my "self worth" bank!

My Self Worth Bank

What you do and how you live matters to God, because you matter to Him and so do the people who need our help. One way He will evaluate our lives will be according to the way we invest ourselves in the poor and needy. He appreciates what we do for those less fortunate than ourselves, and will reward us for it.

We live in a "look good-feel good" culture, so it's easy to miss the point that a "God culture" is all about "being good-doing good." Want to know the path to joy? "To act justly and to love mercy and to walk humbly with your God" (Micah 6:8). Solomon shares his own life experiment in this regard.

"I said to myself, 'Let's go for it—experiment with pleasure, have a good time!' But there was nothing to it, nothing but smoke" (2:2, MSG). Another translation reads, "Laughter is silly. What good does it do to seek pleasure?" (NLT). It's not that we shouldn't seek pleasure and laughter at all, but rather we shouldn't seek *only* those things.

A God culture is a "see that good is done to others" culture. You can have fun doing that! It's a different kind of fun than the tinsel triviality of silliness. Deep joy that cannot be troubled by trouble is found in doing justice where there is no justice being done; loving mercy where cruelty rules; and walking humbly with your God instead of drawing attention to your good deeds.

I was a very selfish teenager. Looking back, I can't understand how I had any friends! I remember one day in French class I was acting up and being disruptive. My teacher stopped the whole class and said to me in front of everyone, "Jill Ryder, you must be the most selfish creature on God's green earth!" I turned bright red and was totally humiliated and angry at her, but I knew she was right. I thought I was making a lot of fun for my friends and me—but actually I deserved the rebuke. It got me thinking that I ought to put my time to more profitable use!

But try though I would, I could not get that egocentricity out of my life. It took the saving life of Christ to get me thinking about others rather than myself. It may not sound like much fun, but joy comes through knowing the Living God who gave Himself for us. He wants to give Himself—through us—to help others.

Satisfaction comes from the experience of getting down and dirty in the ditch with the person who's been beaten up by life on this crazy planet. It's in binding up the man's wounds, putting him on your own donkey, taking him to a place of safety, looking after him until he heals—and paying the innkeeper's bills on top of it all—that you find purpose! (see Luke 10:30-35).

As you tend to the physical needs of one beaten up by robbers, joy comes in telling them that they are made for another world—a world where there will be no more pain, tears, death, sickness, poverty or despair. There is great joy in promoting justice, mercy, and grace in a world where, as in Qoheleth's world, injustice lives in the courts and cruelty survives in the streets.

It's "No Fair"

"And I saw something else under the sun: In the place of judgment —wickedness was there, in the place of justice—wickedness was there" (3:16). Later the Teacher comments, "There is something else meaningless that occurs on earth: righteous men who get what the wicked deserve, and wicked men who get what the righteous deserve" (8:14). What's more he warns, "God will bring to judgment both the righteous and the wicked" (3:17).

Have you ever said, "It's not fair"? You're right, life isn't always fair. It stopped being fair in the garden the day of the Fall. Yet God has put a sense of what is right and what is wrong—what is fair—deep down in our being. What's fair and unfair raises its voice inside us, so even a small child will appeal to some unseen yet known standard of right and wrong.

When our two children Judy and David were in kindergarten, David hated to sing. One day their teacher in the small one-room schoolhouse asked the children if they would like to sing. Most responded "Yes!"

"Put your hand up if you *don't* want to," the teacher demanded. David put his little hand up. "Good," he thought, "she's going to tell me it's all right if I don't join in."

"Go and stand in the corner!" the teacher thundered at David. He did, and stayed there throughout the class. Judy was horrified. Watching her brother standing there, his little face to the wall, her five-year-old mind saw the injustice of it. She got to her feet, the tears running down her face. "It's no fair! It's no fair!" The teacher turned a wrathful eye upon David's little sister and said, "What's no fair?"

"You asked him if he wanted to," the little girl replied. "You asked him if he wanted to sing, and he told you!"

Good point, Judy! She was still sobbing when I picked the kids up that afternoon. We all need to do a little more sobbing, I think! There is injustice in the world at every level and we need to address it at every level.

Why does God allow it when He has the power to stop it? you may ask. Finding myself facing that question like so many others on

9/11, I resorted to a verse in Deuteronomy: "The secret things belong to the LORD our God, but the things revealed belong to us and to our children forever" (29:29).

One thing He has revealed is that life here on earth will be full of injustice and sorrow until He has made a new earth where righteousness reigns. Jesus Himself said, "In this world you will have trouble. But take heart! I have overcome the world" (John 16:33). We who profess to know the Lord are to live rightly in a "wrongly" world! To shine as lights in the darkness and do our level best to point out inequities.

"Will not the Judge of all the earth do right?" (Genesis 18:25). Yes indeed, He will! He will bring everything to judgment. Meanwhile, we need to do right too!

GRAFT IN THE MARKETPLACE

In a world where justice doesn't seem to rule, envy and malice abound instead of trust and esteem. We do not trust that we will "get what we deserve" since the world isn't fair, so we spin our wheels being resentful of what "others" have. The Teacher remarks, "I saw that all labor and all achievement spring from man's envy of his neighbor" (4:4). In other words, "most people are motivated to success because they envy their neighbors" (4:4, NLT).

If we could define envy it would be someone saying, "I want what you've got." If it's not checked—repented of and replaced with kindness and goodness, it can grow into deep bedrock jealousy where it grows horns and says, "I'm angry that I don't have what you've got—and I don't want you to have it either!" In our own minds, we pervert the idea of justice as if it means we *deserve* to have whatever our neighbor has!

Saul envied David. He envied David's popularity with women and his obvious favor with God, a favor Saul had lost by playing the fool. He looked at David and said, "I want what he's got." This grew unchecked into a murderous jealousy, the type Shakespeare called the "green eyed monster." Saul ended up saying, "I want what he's got and what's more, I don't want him to have it at all!" Thereupon he threw his spear at David to try and kill him.

Solomon, David's son, also saw tremendous envy and coveting going on, leading to all sorts of cruelty, jealousy and violent behavior. "Again I looked and saw all the oppression that was taking place under the sun: I saw the tears of the oppressed—and they have no comforter; power was on the side of their oppressors—and they have no comforter" (4:1). As Solomon watched his world he saw lots of tears, for lots of reasons—and it devastated him.

Outrageous Violence

"I turned my attention to all the outrageous violence that takes place on this planet" is the way the same verse reads in *The Message* (4:1). Pick up your newspaper. What do we see? Outrageous violence. Tonight I turned on the television. It was just a normal day on planet earth. A group of teenagers had been arrested for allegedly plotting a killing spree in their school. In Iraq, insurgents had just blown up a mosque killing nearly a hundred people. In our city a ten-year-old was arrested in the beating death of a man. A predator had snatched a child from her bedroom in the middle of the night and tortured her. This—all in one newscast. There was no time left for any good news because of all the "outrageous violence." It seems evil reigns unchecked in our day as it did in Solomon's. What's more, says Solomon, "The oppressors have great power, and their victims are helpless" (4:1, NLT).

I have seen outrageous violence all over the world—here in the United States and in Asia, Africa, Eastern and Western Europe; in the Middle East and everywhere else I go! Power indeed appears to be on the side of the oppressors. I have echoed Solomon's words: "I concluded that the dead are better off than the living" (4:2, NLT). "It is all so meaningless and depressing," says Quoeleth (see 4:8). Is that your reaction?

Or—do you ask God what can be done about it, and what is your personal part of the "doing"? Do you open your mind to ideas He might bring you? Even something small like speaking out at a town meeting or writing to a newspaper could make a difference. It could be costly to open our mouths, but if we don't, the time may come when there is no one to open their mouth for us!

As the Third Reich died at the end of the Second World War, many were trying desperately to assassinate Hitler. (German historians have documented forty-two plots on Hitler's life—all failed.[1]) Martin Niemöller and Dietrich Bonhoeffer joined the underground in an attempt to kill him. Both spoke out publicly against the hell that Hitler had created, knowing that to speak out could be their death sentence. Both were caught and Bonhoeffer was executed by hanging. Niemöller, imprisoned in the Sachsenhausen and Dachau concentration camps, is said to have written these famous words:

> First they came for the Jews
> and I did not speak out because I was not a Jew.
> Then they came for the Communists
> and I did not speak out because I was not a Communist.
> Then they came for the trade unionists
> and I did not speak out because I was not a trade unionist.
> Then they came for me and there was no one left
> to speak out for me.[2]

When we see the seeds of violence and injustice, we need to speak up! Staying silent might not save those you love or even yourself, and in fact may get you into a whole lot of trouble. We are to speak up for those who are weak or helpless and cannot speak up for themselves.

This may seem to be a daunting task. Are you scared? Are you worried about what to say? We need to be in touch with God. First, He will give us courage. Then He gives us words. Jesus said when we are brought before kings, God will give us in that very hour the words to speak. We are not to worry, but do what is right! (see Matthew 10:18-20).

Sometimes we don't want to speak out against evil because we buy into the idea that says, "Don't snitch." It's common for teens in our society to be aware of other kids obtaining drugs. They could speak up, but consider it disloyal. Snitching is out! They're also afraid of the consequences from their friends if they tell. But if they really want the best for all concerned, they would do what is right and speak out to save other kids from getting into worse, possibly harmful or fatal, trouble.

Life's a Beach

In fact unrestrained evil can overwhelm us and make it difficult to speak. Job 29 says, "the chief men refrained from speaking and covered their mouths with their hands; the voices of the nobles were hushed, and their tongues stuck to the roof of their mouths" (verses 9-11). Our fear and anxiety can make it feel like our tongues are stuck! We need to believe, one, there will be a final accounting and until then we do our part. Two, God will give us hope and courage even when the whole situation seems hopeless. And three, we must lift up our heads and trust we will see somewhere at some time in some place, the "goodness of the LORD in the land of the living" (Psalm 27:13).

The devil, who is prince of this world, is busy stirring up social chaos but wants us distracted so we don't do anything about it. But even though the devil is the prince of this world, Jesus is the King! So when the evil one hands us a pair of blinkers we need to resist his promptings, open our eyes to the situation, and tune in to the voice of the Holy Spirit instead.

The devil is the master of delusion and confusion. *God is turning a blind eye to injustice,* he says, *so why should you bother?* Go ahead and let the world cry. Keep out of trouble. Stay away from people's pain. If you hear a child's cry ignore it; if you see a man starving pass on by. If you witness blatant injustice distract yourself. Don't ask for trouble. "Life is a beach!" he shouts in our ear, and keeps asking anxiously, "Are we having fun yet?" Don't get involved in his mantra!

We who profess to align ourselves with the King and His kingdom here on earth should pray daily, "Thy Kingdom come! Thy will be done—as in heaven, so on earth!" If we remain silent in the face of gross injustice and refuse to raise our voices in protest, then when our turn comes to be the victim we may find, as Niemöller warned, there is no one left to defend us.

Our enemy uses pleasures as well as pain to distract us from other people's needs, including the pleasure of relationships. We want to matter to our friends, so how can we speak the truth in love if we see them doing something wrong? When our enemy sees us seeking significance and needing to matter to someone, he tries assuring us, "You matter to someone—you matter to me! I want you to come home to my place. Sleep over! I want to play with you here so I can play with you there."

If pleasure doesn't distract us, pain and relationships will. As God allows troubles to come our way, we can be overwhelmed. Yet meaning is found in opening our eyes to injustice and trying to speak up about it. Satisfaction comes in trying to stop wickedness and stepping in to protect the innocent from abuse and violence, even if we get ourselves hurt in the process. It's called taking up your cross and following Him.

USE THE INFLUENCE YOU HAVE

Solomon was king and had the power to do something about the courts, the crime and the crying. He had the resources to mend the torn, heal the sick and appoint honest judges and administrators over the people. But for a time he just put in "pleasure ear plugs" and used his God-given riches, wisdom and power to indulge himself, feed himself, satiate himself and please himself. He turned a deaf ear to the problems of his people.

Before I condemn him, however, I have to ask myself, "Well, Jill, you have lots of resources too! You have some power and influence. You write books and give talks. To what end?"

Do I write books to write books, and give talks to give talks? What do I write about? Do my writings prick the consciences of those who read them? What do I do that makes a difference in a hurting world? Do I just talk about it or do I take action?

I was being challenged by the words in Isaiah 58. He explains the kind of fasting that means something to God: "To share your food with the hungry and to provide the poor wanderer with shelter —when you see the naked, to clothe him, and not to turn away from your own flesh and blood" (verse 7). It led me to look around for an organization that cared for the poorest of the poor. I joined the board of World Relief, Inc. years ago, and found myself in a whole new world. I began to use my tears, my time, my resources and gifts to practically help the needy.

If you are a teacher, keep your eyes open for ways to intervene in trouble brewing; if you're a nurse, watch out for those without visitors and perhaps pick up the slack yourself. If a neighbor is in trouble, walk across the yard and offer to help in any way you can. It's not that hard to get involved. In fact, it's a daily choice!

Somewhere along the line Solomon repented of his misuse of the resources with which God had blessed him and gave himself to "being good" and "doing good" for the remainder of his life. I don't know if Solomon ever joined an organization like World Relief, but when he returned to God and reorganized his priorities he began to rule and reign in justice and wisdom and put some of these things right. After all, it had been his intention from the start. Hadn't he asked God in the dream for justice and wisdom to rule the people of God? And God had given him wisdom to rule judiciously and well. God also gave him the gift of words to command justice.

VISITING JESUS IN PRISON

A few years ago I was offered an opportunity to join a team of volunteers to go to a prison and speak to the inmates. I had done a bit of prison ministry here and there, but this was different. I would speak at the chapels and to the volunteers. I had an incredible time, not least in my own heart!

My part on the team of volunteers was to speak in the chapels with mostly "lifers," as they're called. I was a new recruit in this ministry. Imagine you were me and had to give an hour's message in one of these chapels. What would you say? That's right, a whole hour! I have to tell you it stretched me to the max, but I wouldn't have missed the chance to join the team because I could hear a whisper in my soul, "I was in prison and you visited me!" (see Matthew 25:36). Do you know what that is worth?

OFFERING JESUS A ROSE

So what did I talk about for a whole hour? Prayer. That's something all of them have time enough to do on the inside. But like many of us on the outside, they don't know how to do it.

Specifically I talked about praying for their families. The greatest punishment for these women is separation from their families and especially their kids. Some have periodic visits from their relatives. Others told me, "I haven't seen my kids for three years" (or more). Our team prayed for their children and encouraged the inmates to pray for them too. We told them they didn't have to wait for a chaplain to visit their cell to pray for them. The tears flowed from the eyes of prisoners and volunteers alike.

Many of these women have found Christ. Many have not. All of them want to know how to find God in their incarceration and talk to Him. I had the joy of teaching a workshop on prayers they could pray themselves back in their cells. I taught them an acrostic for PRAY: Praise—Repent—Ask for others—Yourself.

The ladies wanted to know more about how to praise Him. They also had been telling us that "birthdays are the worst!" That's when they really agonize for their kids. And then there's Christmas! When you can never get home for Christmas, the heartache is sharp and just won't quit. Imagine. That's when I shared with them the story about "the roses." I was deeply moved that it had such an impact on them. I'll share the story with you here.

I was at a meeting in Singapore, where a veteran missionary had shared an experience on the mission field. It was about trying to get home, not for Christmas but for his mother's ninetieth birthday. Because of a crisis and the primitive circumstances in which he worked (he had a leadership role in the mission), it was impossible to get away. It broke his heart.

That must have hurt, I ruminated as I listened to him. How difficult both for him and his mother. It hurts so badly when we or those we love can't get home for the holidays. Well, I thought, at least Jesus will be home for Christmas this year! He wasn't always able to make it. For thirty-three years it was impossible. He had a leadership role in The Mission!

The missionary told us how he had the brilliant idea of sending his mother ten roses each hour of her birthday until she had received all ninety. He tied a thank you note to each rose and sent her a card with the first batch of ten. It said, "How do I love you—let me count the ways." Then he thought of ninety ways he loved his mother and attached a thank-you to every rose!

A while later I was back home from Singapore and it was nearing Christmas. The hustle and bustle of shopping, decorating, and preparing for guests was wearing me out. I needed some time alone with my Savior, and specifically I wanted to spend some time praising Him. I thought about this missionary and his roses. "I'll do that," I decided. So I bought a big bunch of roses and sat down to talk to Him. I call this special place — this conversing with my Savior — the Deep Place Where Nobody Goes. (In fact, I even wrote a book with that title. This story is in that book.)

As I stayed quite still in the Deep Place, I could hear angels singing carols — practicing. Pretty.

"Hullo." I jumped. It was Jesus.

"Oh! Hullo. I thought I'd get ahead of the rush," I told Him. He looked at the roses in my hands and I resisted the urge to give Him the whole bunch at once and return to the mall to continue my shopping — I did have a busy day ahead of me.

I began taking the roses one by one and carefully attaching a message to each. Then I said, "How do I love Thee — let me count the ways." And I began to count them. I wanted above all to thank Him that He had been willing *not* to get home for Christmas for thirty-three years so that one day *I* could!

He sat there, relaxed (He must have done all His shopping already), and He looked serious and focused. (I love that.) He accepted each offering into His hands. I tried not to look at the scars. (I hate that.)

"I love you for sitting with me in the Deep Place Where Nobody Goes," I began, handing Him a flower. "And I love it that you always follow me away from this place and remind me you are in The Shallow Place where everyone lives — even though I forget you're there in all the commotion. And I love you for coming to earth and walking straight into my heart — and making this woman yours forever. And, oh, how I love you for becoming poor so I could become rich beyond measure. Yes, yes, Lord; that I—through your poverty—could become rich! I love you, I love you, I love you!"

Rose by rose I thanked Him, telling Him all the ways I loved Him, and then the bunch of flowers were in His hands and mine were empty. I cried—happy grateful tears, and watched in amazement as each tear became a rose petal strewn around His feet.

He bent down holding my roses carefully, gathering my flowers of love and thankfulness into His scarred hands, saying quietly, "Not one of these shall fall to the ground." Then He looked at me with eyes so full of love I thought I would die. Then He was gone.

I heard the church bells ringing then, and knew I had to return to The Shallow Place where everyone lives. I did so reluctantly knowing the party was about to begin—Christmas was coming![3]

A Great Gift

That was the story I told the women in the prison. I received an e-mail from the leader of this wonderful prison ministry, "Discipleship Unlimited," after the week's work. It said, "Tonight as we visited the women a week after your visit, the women were sharing about the roses. How that story impacted them. They are presenting roses to Jesus. I was amazed at the depth of the sharing tonight. They talked about the questions you had after the bombings (in the UK as a child in World War Two) . . . and shared they had those same thoughts living in abusive homes. They were so honored that you would teach for one hour. It was a great gift to them."

I couldn't help but think how an hour's teaching would be received in our women's conferences or churches these days. And if I had been asked to talk for so long—I can't imagine anyone thanking me for this "great gift" to them!

Linda's e-mail told me the prisoners were busy offering Him their roses day by day in their tiny cells. Should we do less? It's quite easy. Start with the words, "How do I love Thee? Let me count the ways . . . one, two, three . . . "

All of us can look around and ask the Lord to show us people in trouble, needing assistance, encouragement and practical help in this less than perfect world. We have a choice to use our influence wherever we are and whoever we are. We are instruments of His justice, if we will just accept the responsibility! After all, the mission field is between our own two feet at any given time.

FOR GROUP OR PERSONAL STUDY

Quietly MIND MANAGE these concepts:

1. How can we make a significant difference? By living a significant life, directed by a significant God. How are you doing in this area of life?

2. Read Ecclesiastes 9:13-18. Do you have to be rich and famous to make a difference in society? What strikes you from this passage? What is encouraging? Discouraging?

3. Why is it so hard to speak up against injustice? Do you agree that getting involved is a choice? What stops us?

Discussion or Journal

1. Read some examples of what the Bible says about the people God thinks are significant. How does God feel about them?
   Psalm 132:15
   Psalm 146:9
   Proverbs 11:11
   Isaiah 61:1-3

2. What did God expect of His people? See the following verses:
   Deuteronomy 15:4
   Exodus 22:21-23
   Exodus 23:6
   Psalm 72:4

3. Read Ecclesiastes 8:14 and 3:16. Discuss the main thought from these verses.

4. Read Ecclesiastes 4:1. What does this teach us about the perpetrators? The victims? Solomon?

Pray for Yourself and Others

- Pray for the poor and oppressed.
- Pray for victims and perpetrators of violence.

- Pray for the strength and courage to get involved.
- Pray that God will bring you opportunities to get involved.

Carry Out

Ask yourself, "Am I giving a significant amount of my time, prayer, money and heart to intentionally involve myself in areas I can help? Am I giving my life away? What am I doing socially? How, when, where?

Decide *today* where you will take action *tomorrow*!

MAKING CHOICES

*I saw the tears of the oppressed—and they have
no comforter; power was on the side of their
oppressors—and they have no comforter.*

ECCLESIASTES 4:1

Hear them crying, hurting dying,
None to help or care;
All around us, will they find us
Cold and unaware?
Will we reach them, tell them, teach them
See them come alive?
Clothe them feed them, house them lead them
Watch them grow and thrive.

Violence ending, mercy sending
Caring for the poor;
Justice dealing, stopping stealing
Outside our front door.
Raising voices, making choices
We will help and give:
Love and caring, costly sharing,
Christ for You we'll live!

Jill Briscoe

CHAPTER 8

SEARCHING FOR SPEAKING SKILLS

That Will Change My World

Not only was the Teacher wise, but also he imparted knowledge to the people.

ECCLESIASTES 12:9

The Teacher had *wisdom plus skill*, a powerful combination. He had skills that could change his world! What were they? Solomon was a great speaker and a writer. He had *word skills*. Once he returned to God, he also had a heart to commit what was left of his life to making a difference. He stopped being self-centered and began to be other-centered. He used his word skills in the service of God.

What weapons did Solomon use to fight wrong-doing? We don't know if he cleaned up the courts and sorted out his justice system. We don't know if he started a new program to care for widows and orphans, or made his soldiers patrol the streets and get the violence under control. But we do know he used a very powerful weapon — the weapon of words.

Words can be wonderful or terrible things! We can use them to build up or break down. To bring hope, laughter, or tears. We can encourage one another when we speak the truth into our friends' lives. We can express compassion, love and understanding. Words are powerful! There are so many godly ways we can use our words, including directly speaking the gospel message. In some ways, we are all teachers. Like Solomon, we can use our words to pass along the lessons we have learned. We might be a mom or a dad, a school teacher or youth leader, an influencer or simply a friend — but no matter what our position in life, we can use our "word skills" to share love and share the gospel message.

The Words of the Wise Are Like Goads — and Nails!

Many people have wisdom and word skills but keep them to themselves. Others aren't sure what their talents and gifts are. The Teacher knew who he was, how God had endowed him, and that he had the gift of words. He also knew this endowment was not for his enjoyment only, but that he had been blessed in order to be a blessing. He taught truth to his generation, passing on the knowledge of God and His ways. He didn't hoard his words but rather used them as powerful weapons to convince people of the truth about God. In Ecclesiastes 12:11 he tells us, "The words of the wise are like goads, their collected sayings like firmly embedded nails—given by one Shepherd."

His words were described as goads and nails. The goad was the sharp instrument used to prod obdurate cattle into compliance—to move a beast from one place to the next. Words of wisdom are like that. They can move people from non-belief to belief; from secular thinking to spiritual thinking. He also describes these words as given by "one Shepherd." We get them straight from God.

So what are we doing with the knowledge of God that *we* have? Are we asking God to show us how to pass on the truth about Him to our own generation, or are we just building great warehouses in which to stack all that knowledge we have received? Have we discovered the endowment of God in our lives—our talents, gifts, and opportunities? I believe, as the Teacher says, that one day we will be held to account for what we did with our life and skills, and in particular all those words.

Solomon used the wise words given by God to instigate belief in the unbeliever and hope in the follower; as well as to inspire, instruct and challenge both. And he used his God-endowment like none before or after him.

Think about it. How do we use words? What do we talk about

all day long? If we could count up the thousands of words we use every day, how many would be about God—or at least godly? Do our words "goad" people in the right direction, prick their consciences? Move them from meaninglessness to meaningfulness? From nothingness to something-ness? From nonsense to God-sense?

In Solomon's time, nails were tent pegs that gave a tent structure and form. That's what words of wisdom do. When words explain the deep purpose and meaning a relationship with God gives us, they add substance to a person's life. They inform, inspire and instruct. So the result of godly lives infused with wisdom, added to skill and enterprise, is people who are willing to live their lives in good shape! The wise man or woman uses words to proclaim the gospel.

Words of wisdom will not be ignored. They are loud, making their presence felt. They rise above the cacophony of noise in our hurried world and shout out that life is to be lived for God.

I have met many people who have lived their lives and used their words "out loud" even in places where to do so is a dangerous thing and brings down wrath upon their heads. These are people who realize that with the privilege of "God knowledge" comes the responsibility to inform the public of this vital information.

This should be easy to understand. We live in America where the public's "right to know" is almost sacred. We feel we have an inalienable right to know anything that happens—whether or not it affects our lives and well-being! How much more do people have the right to know about things that *will* affect their *eternal* well-being?

LIVING YOUR LIFE OUT LOUD

Back in my study in Wisconsin after an exciting ministry tour in Asia, I was thinking about all the Lord's people we had met whose lives are lived "out loud" in really troublesome situations. They insist on such a vibrant life in Christ that their lives shout the message of transformation to their world just by being who they are. They want as many people as possible to hear them, even though they could get into big trouble by verbalizing their faith and announcing how much they love Jesus. It's pretty impressive!

And whenever they have the chance, they use words to explain their lives to those who watch them. They tell others where their power and life skill come from, and by Whose help they live and move and have their being. Some of these people have told me that their good lives draw attention in the middle of a corrupt world and they need to explain it, lest a mistake be made and people think it is by their own power and godliness that they live.

Both their testimony and the Teacher's words concerning the brevity and importance of time on this little swinging planet have reinforced in me the necessity of "redeeming the time, because the days are evil" (Ephesians 5:16, KJV). This experience of meeting and listening to teachers from all over the planet, whose words are like goads and nails, has made my speaking and writing, evangelizing and discipling, somehow more urgent. "Brief, brief" is the time.

Goading people from secular thinking to belief in the one true God is His work, but He has chosen to involve those of us who love Him in the task. And He is not like the Egyptian taskmaster who gave the Israelites orders to make bricks but didn't give them straw! (see Exodus 5:7). He has given us straw—the skills to do it.

I remember during the Second World War a poster that dominated most billboards. It was a life-size picture of Winston Churchill pointing at us and saying that Britain needed us to join in the war effort. At the same time Churchill talked to Eisenhower and asked for help. "Give us the tools and we'll finish the job," he said. England had a lot of courage and was game to fight but had no weapons! America helped and gave us the tools.

God doesn't tell us to fight the good fight without supplying us with weapons. He doesn't tell us to make bricks without straw. He gives us tools: skills, gifts and talents. Some of those powerful weapons or tools are wise words.

Words Are Weapons for Good or for Ill

As a child of the war years I can remember some perfect examples of the potential of words to be used for good or evil. I read Hitler's words (fueled by the evil one) that set his nation on the path of destruction. His speeches were mesmerizing; his passion and flow of words frighteningly effective. I also listened to Churchill use words to rally the rest of the world to stop him. Goads and nails! Words are a mighty force for good or evil—for God or Satan, for nonsense or God-sense.

The Teacher tells me there is a God to know and obey who will give us the tools we need to fight against Satan and all his minions. In knowing Him, even in a violent world, we can live our lives "out loud" and unafraid, like my friends living in troublesome places. Whatever our circumstances, He will gift us with natural talents and spiritual abilities to "finish the job."

For the rest of this chapter I will be sharing with you the principles from Ecclesiastes 12 that have helped me. I trust they will help you too—so we can all together live our lives out loud. As Jesus said, "As long as it is day, we must do the work of him who sent me. Night is coming, when no one can work" (John 9:4).

The "Know How" to "Know What" to Say

In chapter 2 we discussed the concept of wisdom—how we find it and why we need it. Wisdom, as we noted, is *spiritual intelligence.* Being spiritually "street smart" is impossible without the Spirit of wisdom Himself. In this complicated and heartbreaking world, we need not only *words* but we need the "know how" to "know what" to say—or what not to say! So the first thing we need when we're looking for the right words is wisdom. We have a choice to pick up the tools God offers us, hone our skills and discipline ourselves to be single-mindedly occupied with the war effort.

Perhaps your family is in such a mess you have no stomach for any more fights. There is too much going on inside the four walls of your domicile to even think about the world outside those same four walls! You need wisdom and word skills inside the home as much as outside it. Perhaps even more! How do you face off with a rebellious teenager bent on self-destruction? What do you say to an aging parent who needs elderly care in an institution but refuses to talk about it? What do you do when your teenage son comes out of the closet at the family gathering? We need wisdom and words beyond ourselves at those moments.

We need a spiritual perception and intelligence—God-sense—to deal with relationships that go astray in a family, a mission or in church, as well as in the world at large. The "sword of the Spirit, which is the word of God" (Ephesians 6:17) is needed to broker peace in society—between warring saints, or between beloved but difficult people in our lives. As someone has said:

> *To live above with saints we love*
> *Oh, that will be glory.*
> *To live below with saints we know*
> *—well that's another story!*[1]

Wise words come out of wise people, and I have discovered as Solomon teaches that there is no shortcut. It takes a decision to *work to be wise*! Then we use words to pass along that wisdom where it is desperately needed.

Spiritual Intelligence Takes Spiritual Industry

"The Teacher searched to find just the right words, and what he wrote was upright and true" (12:10). We have to be willing to *work* at finding "just the right words" so that whatever we write or speak is upright and true. The words don't fall from the sky. *Wisdom is work.* It doesn't come naturally—it comes spiritually. The teacher of wisdom wearies himself or herself, pondering and contemplating wise words to impart to the next generation; searching them out until fitting words are found.

The idea is that we should speak words of charm and color. God can help us say things in a disarming way, and color our speech so that it is not just black and white. It takes work to find the *right way* to say the right words.

I think of a time I had received some very bad news as I was about to leave for a speaking engagement in another city. I was still reeling from the information, and just as I stepped out the door to go to the airport, the phone rang again. I hesitated, wondering whether to let it ring, but stepped back in the house and picked it up. It was a spiritually intelligent friend of mine from the other side of the country.

"What's wrong?" she asked.

"What do you mean?" I answered.

"Something's wrong!" she said. "I couldn't get you off my mind."

I told her quickly about the news I had just received, and how it had distressed me. Then she said, "Don't waste the pain—let it drive you to God, not away from Him." That was all, but it was enough. These were wise words like nails, hammering my tent into good shape and keeping me firmly in place. While I was on the plane, I spent time with the Shepherd and wrote:

> *Don't waste the pain, let it prove Thee*
> *Don't stop the tears, let them cleanse thee,*

Rest: stop the striving; soon you'll be arriving in His arms.
Don't waste the pain, let it drive thee deeper into God,
He's waiting—And you should have come sooner!

I was able to let my friend's words "goad" me in His direction.

God wants us to be ready at any time of the day or night to speak into people's pain and trouble. We need to be working ahead of the game on our spiritual growth and understanding, placing wise hopeful concepts in our "help bank" so when we need to draw some out, we don't come up empty. If this sounds like a whole lot of work—you're right! Words that work are words that have worked! As the Teacher says, "Much study wearies the body" (12:12). Solomon *worked* to find the right words.

"He pondered and searched out and set in order many proverbs" (12:9). When it says he *pondered*, it means he worried it out! He worked hard with text, ideas and illustrations. He tried to understand other people's wisdom too, sifting out the true wisdom to be found.

As I come to the Bible, I read the text and then set to work pondering. And work it is! Then like the Teacher who studied and researched the subject, I gather the things learned and set them in order or "catalogue" them. And remember, the Teacher didn't have computers to do it for him like we have. He didn't even have a typewriter!

For years I wrote longhand. In fact I wrote over forty books that way. I had never learned to type and was intimidated by the idea of computers. If you are in a position in which you do not have skills, tools or instruments, I want to encourage you. If you can read and write, then set to and do it anyway. Don't think, "If I don't have a secretary or typewriter or computer, I can't teach or preach effectively." Solomon managed—as did nearly every teacher and preacher throughout all of time up until the late twentieth century! We can too.

"The Teacher searched to find just the right words, and what he wrote was upright and true" (12:10). He achieved his goal. He got to the heart of the truth of the matter he was looking for, but not before a whole lot of work had gone into it. Then it took a whole lot more work getting it in shape to share with the world. The Teacher spared no pains in seeking truth and comprehension. Then the task of organizing all of that into transferable form was even more hard work! But it was infinitely worthwhile.

SERVING UP OTHER PEOPLE'S COOKING

Today we have the Internet where you can pull together a sermon, complete with illustrations, in fifteen minutes. There are catalogues of illustrations to match topics. It's all excellent. But the danger is that the process doesn't always happen in the teacher's mind that way. It can bypass his heart and arrive in the Bible study group or pulpit like pre-packaged supermarket food in plastic containers, instead of homemade cooking.

When we prepare a talk and ponder, research, and catalogue the information ourselves, and it comes from the teacher's heart, I believe it shows in the teacher's eyes and face—and ultimately in the power of the words. You're not serving up someone else's leftovers; you have cooked the whole meal from scratch! It tastes different too! I'm not saying not to use other people's illustrations—I have many times—but they are not the bulk of my teaching. I use a minimal amount, and the rest of the ideas are my own, given to me by the Shepherd.

Years ago when we lived in the UK, Stuart was an evangelist and overseas most of the time. (I felt sad for the people in the UK that were missing out on his wonderful sermons!) I was busy at home with three kids but very involved locally with young people. I put them into preaching teams and took them out on the Methodist circuit —small churches that didn't have any pastors. The Methodist church in Britain in the 1960s had few preachers but a big emphasis on laymen and women doing the work of the ministry.

None of us knew what we were doing but we "had a go" as we say in England. I had never been to Bible school and didn't believe I had a creative bone in my body, so I borrowed other people's ideas, and when it was my turn to preach the sermon I borrowed a sermon too. I always used the same one. It was Stuart's—one of my favorites—about Lazarus.

I can still remember the outline because I preached it over and over! Lazarus was dead; Lazarus was defeated; Lazarus was dangerous! Well, my valiant teenagers and I roamed all over the country area in the English Lake district where we lived, taking Methodist services when we were invited to do so. One time when Stuart was home he took off to preach down in Manchester. I was over my head getting three preschoolers ready for Sunday school, so kissed him happily goodbye and it wasn't until half an hour later I stopped dead in the kitchen and said, "Oh, NO!" I remembered that just a month previously I had been in the church he was going to and had preached his excellent sermon on Lazarus! I spent a miserable day, but not so miserable as my poor husband—who preached his sermon anyway.

In the evening he walked into the house and I took one look at his face and asked quietly, "Lazarus?"

"Lazarus!" he replied quite sternly. "Jill, at the end of *my* sermon some woman came barreling up to me and said, 'Oh, you stole your wife's sermon!'" Stuart advised me to go and find my own illustrations and create my own sermons.

"But I'm not creative," I whined. "You go all over the world teaching others how to put talks together but you've never shown me how to do it. Help me."

Stuart looked thoughtful and said, "Put on your coat, we are going for a walk." We walked up and down our country lane and my husband said, "We are staying out here until you have your first creative thought!" It was cold and wet and I wanted to put a move on and get back where it was warm. But try as I would, I couldn't "get" what Stuart was asking me to do.

We came to a bridge over a little stream. We stopped. Stuart dropped a pebble in the water.

"What Bible verse does that remind you of?" he asked. I looked desperately at the ripples. Nothing came to mind.

"Work at it, Jill."

Then as I put my mind to it, I had my first very own illustration. "Acts 1:8," I said triumphantly. "Ye shall be witnesses unto me both in Jerusalem, and in all Judaea, and in Samaria, and unto the uttermost part of the earth."

I watched the widening ripples and had the outline of my talk. The essence was: The gospel must be preached in the entire world by the disciples of Jesus. How do we do it? Start in the center—in Jerusalem (the mission field is between our own two feet), then move out like the ripples to Judea, the area around Jerusalem, then on to Samaria where it's going to get a little tougher, and then out into "the uttermost parts of the world." It wasn't earth shattering but it was "mine" and I was off and running.

CREATIVITY TAKES WORK

"I didn't understand that creativity takes work," I told my delighted husband. (Now I wouldn't be stealing any more of his messages!) It takes a lot of energy to be creative. Yes it does, but all of us are creative in measure—some more than others, but all are made in the image of a creative God. So by all means—use helps, and other people's ideas and illustrations—but only after you have done your own homework and attacked the challenge diligently.

"But I'm not a teacher, preacher or evangelist!" I can hear some of you saying. "I'm just a simple Christian who teaches first grade Sunday school." All the more necessity to take to heart what I have just written. I was not a preacher or evangelist—I certainly had no seminary training. But those who have the privilege of teaching children have to work twice as hard to understand the truth and deliver it in on their level. It is an art to break truth small enough for them to digest!

So what is the secret of finding words that will change the world? And where do I get the power and strength to declare them to the next generation? The secret lies in spiritual intimacy: in willingness, first and foremost, to ask God for your sermons, talks and ideas. Then you have to put in due diligence to shape all the work, with charm and color, into wise and winsome words so you will "win some"!

We need a whole lot more people imparting knowledge. Little people and big people. Black people and white people. Tall people and short people. All people who know and love the Lord! We have a lot of people in the world to tell a lot of people in the world about Jesus! "Let us not become weary in doing good, for at the proper time we will reap a harvest if we do not give up" (Galatians 6:9). Which brings me to a fundamental principle of being skilled and effective in ministry.

My Life Is Only as Powerful as the Time I Spend with God

If I want to declare His power to the people who are living in the shallow places where everyone lives, I need to spend time in the "deep place where nobody goes," receiving ideas and words firsthand from the Shepherd. I have found my life and ministry are only as powerful and rich as the time I spend with God. I must find my way to the "waiting room" a hundred times a day where He is "waiting for me to wait"! I must learn quietude, however much the "busy Grinch" howls. Strangely, in finding quietude so I can hear His voice, I begin to gather words that work so that I can live my life out loud.

However many good things there are to do—good programs to organize, good meals to cook, good children to manage, good soccer games to attend, good messages to prepare and good people to meet—I must above all, work at good intimacy with God. This is where the power lies. Power to live a life of meaning and purpose, and to declare that power to this troubled generation.

So where did the Teacher find all this information? He read other wise men's literature. We can do that! And he looked in the world around him, the world above him and the world within him. That's where we can find the information we need to pass on to others too.

The World Around, the World Within and the World Above

Solomon was given wisdom and insight and a breadth of understanding as measureless as the sand on the seashore (see 1 Kings 4:29). First, he looked in the world around him. The Scripture says that he described plant life, and taught about animals, birds, reptiles and fish. If you read the Proverbs of Solomon, you will see his wise and pithy sayings laced with illustrations from the natural world.

Job was another naturalist who reminded his friends that if they listened to the animals they would learn about God. "But ask the animals, and they will teach you, or the birds of the air, and they will tell you; or speak to the earth, and it will teach you, or let the fish of the sea inform you. Which of all these does not know that the hand of the Lord has done this? In his hand is the life of every creature and the breath of all mankind" (Job 12:7-10).

When Spurgeon gave his lectures to his students he addressed the problem of clergymen without "apparatus" or a library. This was serious for the church men of England in Spurgeon's day, as they were very poor. He suggested they should look around them and they would find all the "windows" (illustrations) for their talks they needed. He said:

If you have no books to try your eyes, keep them open wherever you go, and you will find something worth looking at. Can you not learn from nature? Every flower is waiting to teach you. 'Consider the lilies' and learn from the roses. Not only may you go to the ant, but every living thing offers itself for your instruction. There is a voice in every gale, and a lesson in every grain of dust it bears. Sermons glisten in the morning on every blade of grass, and homilies fly by you as the sere leaves fall from the trees. A forest is a library, a cornfield is a volume of philosophy, the rock is a history, and the river at its base is a poem. Go, thou who hast thine eyes opened, and find lessons of wisdom everywhere, in heavens above, in the earth beneath, and in the waters under the earth. Books are poor things compared with these.[2]

Too Much Talk of Ourselves

Spurgeon also suggested we should glean examples from ourselves. "Even your own faults and failures will instruct you if you bring them to the Lord."[3] Too much talk of ourselves will be too much talk. But in measure, a good example stemming from your own experience might light up a talk here and there. Look within.

Above all, look above all! Look above you, into the face of the One Shepherd. *Words that have worshipped are words that will work.* I have known that fact all my Christian life, and years ago penned a poem that came out of that knowledge.

Give my words wings, Lord
May they fly high enough to reach the mighty
Low enough to breathe the breath of sweet encouragement
Upon the downcast soul.

Give my words wings, Lord
May they fly swift and far
winning the race with the words of the worldly wise
to the hearts of men.
Give my words wings, Lord
See them now, nesting down at Your feet,
Silenced into ecstasy,
Home at last.

Words that work are words that have worshipped. Wise words come out of wise people and there is no shortcut. God has given us the skills we need to do the work of Him who has sent us. We need to do our part.

How do we find out what tools God has given us? Solomon began to rule as king and as events occurred, he responded to them. In the service of his people he discovered he had the skills as he needed them. As we see needs around us and address them, we will discover our gifts. Then we must hone them and practice them. One day at the judgment we will receive our reward.

So in our marriages, ministry, or the marketplace—in the University of Life and the School of Hard Knocks—may God grant us spiritual intelligence gained by spiritual insistence and industry, stemming out of spiritual intimacy—with One Shepherd in the deep places where nobody goes. And may we search and develop all the skills He is waiting for us to use to bless our world.

FOR GROUP OR PERSONAL STUDY

Quietly MIND MANAGE these concepts:

1. Read Ecclesiastes 12:9-12. What has struck you from this passage that has helped you?
2. Think of some pivotal words that have been spoken to you from a wise person. Revisit the incident in your mind. What was said that consoled, challenged or rebuked you? How did God use those words in your life?
3. Do you know what your skills are? Are word skills among them?

Discussion or Journal

1. How much time do you spend getting information from the One Shepherd? Do you feel you might need to spend more time? If so, how might you begin to incorporate this into your life and schedule?
2. What do you think of the concept that "creativity takes work"? In what ways have you worked to stimulate your own creativity? How have you used your creativity for God?
3. What can you do (that you're not doing already) to use your skills in the church, in your family or community, or in the world?
4. Have fun thinking up your own illustration. Choose a verse of Scripture. How could you illustrate it? Look within.

Pray for Yourself and Others

- Spend some extra time with the One Shepherd. Ask Him for whatever words you will need today to make a difference.
- Pray for your pastors, Sunday school teachers, missionaries, evangelists, and Bible study leaders—that they, too, would have wisdom and the right words.

Carry Out

Take a walk outside and choose an object of nature. Consider the birds, for instance, or the stars. What verse comes to mind? How would you explain the Scripture using the example of your chosen object?

LOOKING

The words of the wise are like goads . . . like firmly
embedded nails — given by one Shepherd.

ECCLESIASTES 12:11

Help me Lord to look **above me**
Show me things that I can tell,
From the heavens that will capture
How You manage all things well.

Help me Lord to look **within me,**
Seeing how You've made me whole,
Help me craft them into stories
That will help win people's souls.

Help me Lord to look **about me**
Ever eager to impress
God's good gospel on the listener
Telling them of Ever-ness!

Jill Briscoe

CHAPTER 9

SEARCHING FOR SECURITY

In an Unsafe World

> *"Better to go to a house of mourning than to go to
> a house of feasting, for death is the destiny of every
> man; the living should take this to heart."*
>
> ECCLESIASTES 7:2

Everyone wants to feel safe. I do, don't you? But just how safe and secure are we as we face terrorism, bird flu or dirty bombs? There will, we are assured, be another terrorist attack in the USA. The words that run along the base of our television screens haven't changed for years. They say, *Terror alert elevated.*

There will be more tsunamis in our lives. It's just a matter of time. If it isn't national trouble, it's family trouble. Many of our marriages have grown cold, our kids aren't doing well, and we are struggling with our work, health, weight, and depression. So we are living in this chronic low grade anxiety, waiting for the other shoe to drop. What's more, death in some form or other is all around us. It is more evident, more frightening, more "in your face" than it has ever been. I have found, however, that "death is an evangelist."

DEATH IS AN EVANGELIST

One good thing about 9/11 is that the terrible event has pointedly focused our attention. On what? The inevitability of death! Certainly it has come home to me with great force: we need to be ready to die. That is not at all the same as *wanting* to die.

On September 11th, 2001, I was on a United flight from London to Chicago when the jets hit the World Trade Center. Our flight was diverted to Gander Airport in Newfoundland, where I stayed six days before getting a flight home. Stuart and I boarded a plane to Washington D.C. We were not totally alone on the plane, but pretty near! As we were walking off the jetway and through the airport, we were met by a TV camera crew talking to people about the flight and asking if they were fearful about flying.

Stuart had just asked me a question and was teasing me about my answer and we were laughing together. The TV crew was obviously intrigued, as we were relaxed and enjoying ourselves. So they approached us and asked us a few questions.

"It looks as if you're happy enough flying," the girl reporter commented. I answered, "Well, after my 9/11 experience I guess this was tame." This got her interest and so she got her cameraman to fix his lens on me and said, "Tell me about it." So I told her how scary it had been to be on a United flight on that day and hearing about the attacks; then to be unexpectedly grounded and stuck in the north of Canada for nearly a week. When I had recounted my experience I said, "You just have to be ready to die!" That really got her attention and she asked, "What do you mean?" I gave a nice big smile into the camera and said, "Well, being *ready* to die isn't a bit the same as *wanting* to die. I didn't want to die, but I was ready to die if it was my time." She had had enough of this and so thanked me and moved on.

I thought of Ecclesiastes and the truth of the Teacher's words: "No man knows when his hour will come" (9:12). Death is inevitable in the end, he says, and "the living should take this to heart" (7:2). In other words, death wonderfully focuses the attention on what is really important, and makes you thankful there is a heaven to go to and a Christ to take you there when your time is up.

When we hear of someone we know who has died, doesn't it make you thoughtful? That is why Qoheleth says, "The heart of the wise is in the house of mourning, but the heart of fools is in the house of pleasure" (7:4). When it comes to death there is a lot of nonsense being spoken—and not a lot of God-sense! The Bible tells us we can only go to heaven if we have had the Lord Jesus forgive our sins. How does this happen? We ask Him. Then we bank on the Word of God being truth about the truth of God.

Are you ready to die? If your plane went down today or your car was hit head-on by a drunk driver, or you went to the doctor and received a death warrant, would you be ready? Would you know where you are going? You can know before it happens. In fact it's more than a good idea to find out—and not wait till after the fact! In the end you cannot guarantee your own safety no matter how hard you try and how much money you spend. Don't think just because you go to church you will get a "pass" into heaven!!! Think through the reasons you believe you would go to heaven if you died tonight. Knowing where you're going after death is the greatest—and some would say the *only*—security we have in this unsafe world.

DEATH IS A GREAT LEVELER

Death puts everyone on the same page. Man shares a common destiny—the ground is level in the graveyard. Man indeed "goes to his eternal home and mourners go about the streets" (12:5). The terrorist and the president die. The poor man and the rich man. The black man and the white man. The good man and the bad man. The young man and the old man.

On one trip back home to the UK we took some travel companions to Westminster Abby. There we saw two coffins side by side in places of prominence. They belonged to Mary Queen of Scots and Queen Elizabeth. How ironic that Mary's coffin lay next to Elizabeth's and neither could do anything about it—Elizabeth had had Mary murdered in the Tower of London! Death indeed is a great leveler. "All go to the same place; all come from dust, and to dust all return" (3:20). Remember that Qoheleth is looking at death from the godless perspective and contrasting it with the godly view. The ungodly view is that aging is inevitable and leads to death which is a given, so we should eat, drink and be merry if we can! Death, being an evangelist, says we had better be ready for what comes next.

In Ecclesiastes 12 there is a brilliant description of old age. It is wonderfully humorous—unless it is a picture of you! Usually I can laugh at jokes about aging, except near my birthday. Chapter 12 poetically describes the grim aspects of aging, using a wide variety of amusing metaphors, obvious in their application.

It describes the carefree liveliness of youth fading into a lack of interest in life. This is accompanied by blindness, deafness, and other physical problems. Do we want to offer God the years of our lives *after* we have used up most of our faculties on ourselves?

God wants the best of our lives. The Teacher talks about how hard it is to throw off trouble and anxieties that multiply with advancing age. It's certainly my experience that the older I get the more I find to worry about! The arms and hands tremble, the legs can hardly hold us up. Our teeth fall out and quit grinding our food, and our eyesight fails.

"Men rise up at the sound of birds" (can't sleep past dawn) and we become "afraid of heights and of dangers in the streets." Solomon writes, "The almond tree blooms" as a picture of the white hair of age (12:4-5).

Even a tiny thing like a grasshopper seems unduly heavy (though why one would be carrying one I don't know) and desire (sexual potency) will fail. These vivid pictures depict total collapse. The silver chain from which the lamp hangs is snapped. The golden lamp bowl is crushed. The clay pitcher is broken to pieces so that no water can be brought from the well. The wooden wheel that lowers the bucket into the well has itself been broken (see 12:6).

An interpretation of this set of images links the pictures with parts of the body. The silver cord—the spine; the golden bowl—the head; the pitcher—the heart; and the wheel—the digestive organs.

The body returns to dust. The Old Testament consistently teaches that at death, the life in humans and animals alike returns to God, who is the Giver of life, and after that we humans must give account to God.

So the young man is warned to make the most of life while he has the faculties to enjoy it, remembering that he is accountable to God for the use of all God's gifts. We need to remember our Creator in the days of our youth (see 12:1) before the days come when we are at death's door. But I would add—it's never too late to prepare to meet God. You are never too old to start the long journey to a better home. Every funeral we attend should be an incentive to that end!

Some, however, do not take death to heart, as the Teacher hopes they will. They go straight out of a funeral home and get drunk. Not the way to go! Others become fatalistic and do not allow the sobering reality of death to turn them toward the One they themselves will face one day.

Fatalism says, *If this is all there is, we may as well eat, drink and be merry for tomorrow we die!* Qoheleth reflects this in chapter 3 when he says, "So I saw that there is nothing better for a man than to enjoy his work, because that is his lot. For who can bring him to see what will happen after him?" (verse 22).

The Teacher is echoing the non-believer's point of view again. *Who knows what will happen?* he laments. We know because we have a Bible that tells us we are human beings made in the image of God. People for whom Christ died. If we ever wonder what we are worth, we can remember we were worth dying for. That should give us a sense of self worth!

For those who love the Lord, glory comes after dying, but that does not mean the struggle to get to glory will be easy or pleasant! I'm not a bit worried about the very next moment after death—it's just the way I get to that moment that's scary! It is the process of death itself that is grim.

DENYING DEATH

So it's understandable that we ignore death, pretend it doesn't happen or "live it up" in case *this is all there is*. We have a habit of denying death. We dress death up as if it never happened.

I remember being rather shocked at the way we have wakes in our city when there is an open coffin. I had not experienced this before. As a pastor's wife I long ago began to take my share of responsibilities to visit the dying and attend the funerals of our church people. I discovered that when you looked at the deceased, they could almost look better when they were dead than when they were alive!

At one funeral I was standing by the casket and the relatives were filing past to pay their respects to the deceased man who had died in his seventies or so. "There he is," his sister kept saying over and over again, gazing at the corpse.

"On the contrary," said the widow with spirit. "If I believed *there he was* I wouldn't be able to stand here!" Then in a loud voice, holding onto my hand tightly, she announced to the surprised line of mourners waiting to file by: "There he *isn't*—he's in heaven!" It was quite a dramatic moment.

I reminded that widow of those words as I visited her a good twenty years later as she lay dying. In her hospice bed apparently sleeping, she smiled, and I knew she heard me.

Death has no hold on the one who has trusted God with his or her soul. Certainly the process of death can be grim, but what happens afterward is all glory for the Christian, who enjoys an incredible life lived forever with no more tears, pain, fear or sorrow! The person who has cast themselves on the mercy of God need not fear death. When my own mother died I penned a poem:

HEAVEN

What place is this where rivers flow
And flowers bud and grasses grow?
Where birds compete to praise God's Son,
Where prayers are answered every one.

What place is this where minds at rest
From earth's oppressive battles rest?
Where constant joy is all I know
Where God is everywhere I go?
Where I am overwhelmed to see
The face of Him who died for me!

What place is this where tears are dried
By hands of Jesus crucified?
Where broken dreams are dreamt anew
And come to pass for me for you?
What place, what place, but home to Him
Who'll make me what I might have been

Then I like Christ at last will grace,
The One I worship on my face.
What place is this? It is His throne
I trust you Lord to bring me home![1]

Our God has overcome death—that's what Easter morning is all about!

Death Is Manageable

The fool, the Bible says, has said *no* to God (see Psalm 14:1 and 53:1). The foolish man has every reason to fear, for he has only himself to rely on to save himself after death. If he thinks he is God and can do anything, he will presume he will be able to take care of his eternal soul. How silly is that? How foolish? That's right, it's nonsense, not God-sense. The fool thinks he can be master of his own destiny. To this man even death is manageable. He will find a way to manage death. He goes in for a dangerous game of God-manship.

This person attacks the problem with knowledge. *Science will solve this problem*, he tells us. It's only a matter of time. But no—it is not a matter of time—it's a matter of eternity, and totally in the hands of the God of eternity.

The ungodly man disagrees. *Somehow we have to eradicate death*, he thinks. Man is all-powerful! Man is god. With science he can create life in the laboratory, so one day we will be able to sustain life and eradicate death. This may sound "beyond the pale" to you—but consider this.

Our Culture Says We Can Conquer All — Even Death

"Death is an imposition on the human race and is no longer acceptable. Man has all but lost his ability to accommodate himself to personal extinction. He must now proceed to physically overcome it. In short, to kill death. To put an end to his own mortality as a consequence to being born."[2] This is the opening of a 1969 book that examines the possibility of conquering old age and death, and making people immortal.

Incredible! God sits in heaven and laughs. As a friend of ours said in a sermon, "If you want to make God laugh, tell Him your plans!" Especially your non-funeral plans! How anyone can really believe that man in his genius can eradicate death is beyond me. The Teacher's view of death and dying is much different. He is not buying into this nonsense, but rather understands that death is not "a consequence of being born," but according to the revelation of God, is a result of sin entering the human race. The man who rightly fears a God of reality and revelation will accept the truth that our God has the power of life and death, not any man, no matter how great a scientist he is. As Solomon says, we should "stand in awe of God" (5:7).

What was it that Christ warned us about in the New Testament? "Do not be afraid of those who kill the body but cannot kill the soul.

Rather, be afraid of the One who can destroy both soul and body in hell" (Matthew 10:28). It is God who holds that power note, not Satan!

Ecclesiastes reminds us that "the spirit returns to God who gave it" (12:7). But man without God wants to play God and eradicate death all by himself! He wants to decide where his spirit goes when he dies. He can't do it! This is entirely a God thing.

I remember reading a piece in a newspaper at least forty years ago that went something like this. (I've updated it a little!)

One day a man was having a conversation with God. God said, "I can create a child."

"So can I," sneered the man. "I can make a baby from a sperm and an egg in a test tube."

God said, "I cause flocks and herds to multiply on the earth."

"I can clone a sheep and a pig and a cow," the man said proudly.

"I cause the clouds to form, to gather rain to bless the dry earth," said God.

"That's nothing," replied the man. "I can lace the clouds with silver chloride and make it rain whenever I want too."

"Do you not know I have the power to explode a thousand universes?" murmured God.

"Paltry trick!" snapped the man. "I have made a weapon of mass destruction, and can blow the human race to smithereens."

The man was getting excited. "Watch this!" he shouted. He pressed a button and missiles flew to their prearranged destinations and radiation killed every living thing.

"I can raise the dead," said God.

"Please," pled the man. "Let me live again!"

"Why, who are you?" said God.

Pretty dramatic!

I remember sitting by the body of my mother an hour after she had died. Have you ever seen a dead body? Before it is cared for by the funeral director? That body is so "dead"! I thought to myself. What on earth could bring this "so dead" body of my mother back to life? What power? And fast on the heels of that thought—only God! And the next thought was: Where is my mother? And what is she seeing? I knew she was in heaven, but what was she experiencing? What was it like?

At once this wonderful verse rushed into my mind and settled itself down in my sorrow. "No eye has seen, no ear has heard, no mind has conceived what God has prepared for those who love him" (1 Corinthians 2:9). And Jesus' words to the disciples as He was preparing to walk through death's door for us so we could follow Him to the Father's house, "I am going there to prepare a place for you" (John 14:2).

Jesus will meet us on the other side of death's door. The sobering truth of the matter is that the Bible says when we get through that door God will either say, "I never knew you. Away from me" (Matthew 7:23) or "Well done, good and faithful servant" (25:21). Take your pick.

It's a Terrible Thing to Be Forgotten

As I travel, especially revisiting places we have ministered in for over thirty years, people come up to me and ask, "Do you remember me?" I watch their faces and realize how important it is to them that I remember. But I see so many people, I often can't. I can never bring myself to say, "No, I'm sorry I don't—I've forgotten you!" How horrible that would be. And I'm just Jill Briscoe—no one important! Imagine if God met us the other side of death's door and when we anxiously ask, "Do you remember me?" He says, "No, I'm sorry I don't—I've forgotten you."

It's a terrible thing to be forgotten. It will do no good saying, *but you must remember me. I tipped my religious hat to you at Easter and*

Christmas, and gave money to the United Way. It is too late. So will it be, "I forget you"? or "I forgive you"? Now is the time to make that choice.

Remember the criminal on the cross next to the Lord. "He said, 'Jesus, remember me when you come into your kingdom.' Jesus answered him, 'I tell you the truth, today you will be with me in paradise'" (Luke 23:42-43). Take comfort from this. Up until the very end, it is not too late to make your choice. Death is an evangelist.

How Long Will I Be in the Box?

Thinking about my friend years ago standing by the side of that coffin and announcing triumphantly, "there he isn't," reminds me of an incident some years ago when one of our grandchildren asked his father, "How long will I be in the box?" The child had been watching a funeral on TV and apparently had understood the body of the man who had died was inside the coffin being carried into the church service. Their father took the opportunity to answer, "Not one minute. Absent from the body, present with the Lord" (see 2 Corinthians 5:8). The child asked me the same question as I was putting the kids to bed one night.

The boys had been in and out of the bath, and now were sitting by their beds ready to procrastinate as long as possible before I turned off the light. But I sensed urgency in this little boy. He had obviously been thinking he would not like to die and be put in a box! I tried to find a picture to help him. Looking around the room my eyes fell on the piles of clothes the boys had stripped off and left in two little piles on the floor.

I repeated the quotations their father had given them, and added that Jesus had said, "Whoever lives and believes in me will never die" (John 11:26).

"Then what goes in the box?" the child asked.

"Look here," I said, pointing to the two little piles of clothes on the floor. "This is what will happen when we die. Our bodies will be like the dirty clothes. They will fall off us and *that's* what goes in the box! Meanwhile, the people who lived in the clothes will go to Jesus in heaven. He promises to give us a new body there."

"Oh!" they said. "That's good. So *we* won't be in the box?"

"Right," I replied, "not for one second."

"Life," as Abraham Cowley said, "is an incurable disease."[3] But God has the cure for the incurable—it's called everlasting life. What a message. So for the human being who is born to die, this is good news. Death is a given and death is grim, and even though death is not governable, God offers us eternal life—or the very life of the Eternal One. For the believer in Christ, God has not only put Eternity in our hearts, He has put "The Eternal One" there too if we have asked Him.

To recap, it's "Better to spend your time at funerals than at parties" because a good funeral:

1. Shows our frailty.
2. Forces us to search for God.
3. Reminds us we come from Him and return to Him and there will be an accounting.

So remember Him, advises the Teacher, "before the silver cord of life snaps and the golden bowl is broken. Don't wait until the water jar is smashed at the spring and the pulley is broken at the well. For then the dust will return to the earth, and the spirit will return to God who gave it" (12:6-7, NLT). Remember Him *now* and He will remember you *then*!

It's All True

The families alive in Qoheleth's time had a big advantage over us. We might only visit a funeral home once in childhood, but in his day there was someone sick or dying in every home. The house of mourning was not like the American funeral home, but rather any house where someone had died.

People had no TV, iPods, Blackberries or cell phones to distract them, no gadgetry to occupy their minds, no gracious living to help them to forget. And they had no hospitals to help with the smells, sounds and sight of death.

You died at home in Qoheleth's world (and there are still many cultures where that happens today). The whole family was an integral part of the process. It sort of brings death up close and personal! Even for the children. The next generation needs to understand that, for those who belong to Him, all this is true!

This was brought home to me with new force at a funeral service where I was asked to give the message to the mourners. It was a hard one.

When we first came to the States, Carrie had befriended our daughter. They grew up at our church sharing everything. Both married and both had three kids. Then Carrie was diagnosed with the same disease her mother had died of some years earlier.

I had been out of the country in the last stages of Carrie's brave fight, but when I returned I was told she had chosen to die at home. Would I go to say good-bye?

I remember walking into the room and getting a shock. This young woman, the fourth child of five, was the image of her mother, and suddenly I was back in another death chamber remembering her mother's farewell. Carrie was restless and I stretched out on the bed next to her and prayed and waited. She knew I was there. I prayed that God would help her and settle her spirit down.

When the time came, I said good-bye to Carrie. She could hardly talk. She told me her work was not finished, and she still wanted to tell all who came to her bedside about the Lord, whom she loved to distraction. I assured her she had run a good race, had finished her course well, and had kept the faith. Her work was surely done. Now she could rest.

I told her how much the Lord loved her for her bright faith that was lighting up the room and blessing everyone who came to visit; and for her steady assurance that God was the source of her joy and the Lover of her soul. I thanked her for being a friend to my little girl when we immigrated far away from her home and family years ago. Still she moved restlessly. Then I said, "Carrie, I will be your voice. What do you want me to tell people for you?" In essence she answered me, "Tell them it's all true!"

What did she mean—*it's all true?* She meant the Gospel is true, and that there is a heaven to go to and a Savior to forgive our sin and take us there. She meant the reality and sufficiency of God was really real and sufficient! That even in our death—our "unmaking"—He is all that we need Him to be, *when* we need Him to be. He is all that we need. I promised to tell the world what she would not be able to. It's all true!

And that's what I did at the funeral service, and continue to do, like now. Tell Carrie's and my world it's true. It's real. "He makes everything beautiful in its time." Carrie's home-going was a huge blessing to me as I watched her walk into glory, at peace at last, her unseeing earthly eyes seeing unearthly things that are as yet hidden from me till my turn comes.

Talk about secure! God promises *internal* and *eternal* security for the believer in Jesus; He does not promise always to provide *external* security. But when we are unsafe on the outside, we are safe on the inside and that is what counts. It's all true.

Our wild and frighteningly violent world is all about security.

External security. And I am truly grateful we live in an as yet comparatively safe environment in the West. But as the world darkens in what may well be "the last days," men's hearts will increasingly fail them for fear. The last enemy of mankind—death—will come calling for every one of us. What will we do when our time comes? How will we fare?

Have I put doubts in your mind? Hopefully if I have, it will help you to take time out to sort through what you really believe about death and the afterlife. Even now, why not ask God to show you if anything more needs to be done. Ask Him to forgive your sin and come into your life by His Spirit. If you're not sure you have done that already—do it again! Nothing is lost! Then write the date in your Bible and remember this prayer. Thank Him for doing what He promised to do. Perhaps if you have questions, you may want to have a talk with a pastor. It's too important to dismiss. God wants you to be free from the fear of death. This is why Christ came.

SAFEST OF ALL

I have been in danger on more than a few occasions in my life. After 9/11 Stuart gave me a little note to carry with me in our world travels. It was a quote found on the body of a soldier in the trenches in the Second World War. The man was a well-known English poet. The note said:

Safe shall be my going,
secretly armed against all death's endeavors,
Safe though all safety's lost.
Safe where men fall
And if these poor limbs die
Safest of all!

Sitting high in the skies ever since, I carry the words in my heart. I believe them with all my heart, mind, soul and strength. Do you? "It's all true!" *Safest of all!*

FOR GROUP OR PERSONAL STUDY

Quietly MIND MANAGE these concepts:

1. "Don't let the excitement of youth cause you to forget your Creator. Honor him in your youth before you grow old and say, 'Life is not pleasant anymore.' Remember him before the light of the sun, moon, and stars is dim to your old eyes, and rain clouds continually darken your sky" (Ecclesiastes 12:1-2, NLT). Spend a few moments in prayer and ask yourself the question: If I died tonight where would I go and what will God say to me?

2. What are you most afraid of? What threatens your security? How can you use the ideas in this chapter to overcome your fears?

3. What has been your response to death in the past? How might it be different after pondering Ecclesiastes?

Discussion or Journal

1. What would you say about death to a dying person? What would you say to a teenager? What would you say to an old person who finds it hard to change their mind? Which Scriptures would you turn to?

2. Look up and discuss the verses that speak of Solomon's father David concerning death.
   Psalm 89:48
   Psalm 23:4
   Psalm 56:13
   Psalm 116:8,9,15
   Choose your favorite, write it down. Why does this verse touch you?

Pray for Yourself and Others

- Pray for anyone you know about who is sick or dying.
- Pray for the persecuted church to be willing to suffer death rather than deny Christ.
- Pray for your own family and their eternal well-being.
- Pray for yourself.

Carry Out

Make sure you know the Lord before they "carry you out"!

DEATH'S DOOR

Even though I walk through the valley of the shadow
of death, I will fear no evil, for you are with me; your
rod and your staff, they comfort me.

PSALM 23:4

The door strangely shaped like a cross looms high,
And I try not to look as death walks by,
Then I see a loved figure who takes my hand
And tells me there's glory ahead in His Land.
But there's only one way to the joys ahead,
And that's through death's door
So I don't need to dread,
For death in the end is my friend you see:
For he will release me eternally.
So there's no need to fear what death will do
For he's only God's servant to take you on through!

Jill Briscoe

NOTES

Chapter 1: Searching for Significance

1. C. S. Lewis, *Mere Christianity* (New York: Collier /Macmillan, 1952), 120.
2. C. S. Lewis, *The Great Divorce* (San Francisco: HarperSanFrancisco, 2001), 18.

Chapter 2: Searching for Sense

1. Philip Baker, *Wisdom: The Forgotten Factor of Success* (Australia: Deeper Calling Media, Inc.; New Edition, 2003).

Chapter 3: Searching for a Song

1. Wikipedia, "Philosophy of Søren Kierkegaard," http:// en.wikipedia.org/wiki/Philosophy_of_S%C3%B8ren_ Kierkegaard. Accessed online Feb. 16, 2007.
2. Quoted in Os Guinness, *The Call* (Nashville: W Publishing, 2003), 2.
3. Elizabeth Barrett Browning, Bk. VII, l. 812-826. Accessed online Jan. 20, 2007. Wikipedia: http://en.wikiquote. org/wiki/Elizabeth_Barrett_Browning.
4. "All Good Gifts Around Us Are Sent From Heav'n Above," *Original Trinity Hymnal,* #614. Accessed online Jan. 20, 2007.

http://www.opc.org/hymn.html?hymn_num=614.

5. W. Robinson, *Keswick Hymnbook*, 78.

6. Graham Kendrick and Steve Thompson. Copyright © 1993 Make Way Music, www.grahamkendrick.co.uk. All rights reserved. International copyright secured. Used by permission.

CHAPTER 4: SEARCHING FOR SATISFACTION

1. Online advertisement, Rox Perfumes website. Accessed Jan. 21, 2007. http://www.rox-perfumes.co.uk/shopexd.asp?id=126.

2. BrainyQuote. http://www.brainyquote.com/quotes/quotes/e/ericliddel338714.html. Accessed Feb. 1, 2007.

3. *Random House Webster's Unabridged Dictionary*, Second Edition (New York: Random House, 2001), 163.

CHAPTER 5: SEARCHING FOR SALVATION

1. C. S. Lewis, *Mere Christianity* (New York: Collier /Macmillan, 1952), 120.

2. Wikipedia, accessed February 5, 2007. http://en.wikipedia.org/wiki/Arthur_Stace.

3. Walter C. Kaiser, *Total Life* (Chicago: Moody, 1979), 66.

CHAPTER 6: SEARCHING FOR A SOUL MATE

1. Christian Classics Ethereal Library: Commentary Critical and Explanatory, on the Whole Bible. Accessed online Feb. 5, 2007. http://www.ccel.org/ccel/jamieson/jfb.x.xxi.v.html.

2. *Merriam Webster Unabridged*. Online version. Accessed Feb. 5, 2007. http://unabridged.merriam-webster.com/cgi-bin/collegiate?va=friend.

3. This saying is attributed to numerous different sources, including Charles Spurgeon and Leonard Bernstein.

4. Amy Carmichael, *If* (Oldbury, West Midlands, UK: Christian Literature Crusade, 1999), from the essay "Calvary Love."

5. The Quote Garden: Quotations About Marriage. Accessed online Feb. 14, 2007. http://www.quotegarden.com/marriage.html.

6. Carmichael, *If,* "Calvary Love."

Chapter 7: Searching for Social Justice

1. Roger Moorhouse, *Killing Hitler* (New York: Bantam Books, 2006). Accessed online Feb. 12, 2007. http://www.amazon.com/Killing-Hitler-Roger-Moorhouse/dp/0553803697.

2. Wikipedia, "Martin Niemöller." Accessed online Feb. 15, 2007. http://en.wikipedia.org/wiki/Martin_Niem%C3%B6ller.

3. Adapted from Jill Briscoe, *The Deep Places Where Nobody Goes* (UK: Monarch-Kriegal, 2002).

Chapter 8: Searching for Speaking Skills

1. Jingle of unknown origin, quoted in various sources.

2. C. H. Spurgeon, *Lectures to My Students* (Grand Rapids, Mich.: Zondervan, 1979), 182.

3. Spurgeon, 182.

Chapter 9: Searching for Security

1. Jill Briscoe, *God's Front Door* (UK: Monarch Publishing, 2002).

2. Alan Harrington, *The Immortalist* (New York: Random House, 1969), 5.

3. *The Columbia World of Quotations* (New York: Columbia University Press, 1996). www.bartleby.com/66/. Accessed online Feb. 18, 2007.

ABOUT THE AUTHOR

JILL BRISCOE and her husband Stuart live in Milwaukee, Wisconsin. They have worked together in ministry for over fifty years, and have three grown children and thirteen grandchildren. A native of Liverpool, England, Jill has authored over fifty books. She serves on the board of directors of World Relief and *Christianity Today*, and is editor of *Just Between Us*, a magazine for women in ministry and leadership. Stuart and Jill serve Elmbrook Church as ministers at large, encouraging and training leaders in church and missions around the world.